Perception: A Very Short Introduction

VERY SHORT INTRODUCTIONS are for anyone wanting a stimulating and accessible way into a new subject. They are written by experts, and have been translated into more than 45 different languages.

The series began in 1995, and now covers a wide variety of topics in every discipline. The VSI library now contains over 500 volumes—a Very Short Introduction to everything from Psychology and Philosophy of Science to American History and Relativity—and continues to grow in every subject area.

Very Short Introductions available now:

ACCOUNTING Christopher Nobes
ADOLESCENCE Peter K. Smith
ADVERTISING Winston Fletcher
AFRICAN AMERICAN RELIGION
    Eddie S. Glaude Jr
AFRICAN HISTORY John Parker and
    Richard Rathbone
AFRICAN RELIGIONS
    Jacob K. Olupona
AGEING Nancy A. Pachana
AGNOSTICISM Robin Le Poidevin
AGRICULTURE Paul Brassley and
    Richard Soffe
ALEXANDER THE GREAT
    Hugh Bowden
ALGEBRA Peter M. Higgins
AMERICAN HISTORY Paul S. Boyer
AMERICAN IMMIGRATION
    David A. Gerber
AMERICAN LEGAL HISTORY
    G. Edward White
AMERICAN POLITICAL
    HISTORY Donald Critchlow
AMERICAN POLITICAL PARTIES
    AND ELECTIONS L. Sandy Maisel
AMERICAN POLITICS
    Richard M. Valelly
THE AMERICAN PRESIDENCY
    Charles O. Jones
THE AMERICAN REVOLUTION
    Robert J. Allison
AMERICAN SLAVERY
    Heather Andrea Williams
THE AMERICAN WEST Stephen Aron

AMERICAN WOMEN'S HISTORY
    Susan Ware
ANAESTHESIA Aidan O'Donnell
ANARCHISM Colin Ward
ANCIENT ASSYRIA Karen Radner
ANCIENT EGYPT Ian Shaw
ANCIENT EGYPTIAN ART AND
    ARCHITECTURE Christina Riggs
ANCIENT GREECE Paul Cartledge
THE ANCIENT NEAR EAST
    Amanda H. Podany
ANCIENT PHILOSOPHY Julia Annas
ANCIENT WARFARE
    Harry Sidebottom
ANGELS David Albert Jones
ANGLICANISM Mark Chapman
THE ANGLO-SAXON AGE John Blair
ANIMAL BEHAVIOUR
    Tristram D. Wyatt
THE ANIMAL KINGDOM
    Peter Holland
ANIMAL RIGHTS David DeGrazia
THE ANTARCTIC Klaus Dodds
ANTISEMITISM Steven Beller
ANXIETY Daniel Freeman and
    Jason Freeman
THE APOCRYPHAL GOSPELS
    Paul Foster
ARCHAEOLOGY Paul Bahn
ARCHITECTURE Andrew Ballantyne
ARISTOCRACY William Doyle
ARISTOTLE Jonathan Barnes
ART HISTORY Dana Arnold
ART THEORY Cynthia Freeland

Available soon:

For more information visit our website

www.oup.com/vsi/

Brian Rogers

PERCEPTION

A Very Short Introduction

OXFORD
UNIVERSITY PRESS

OXFORD
UNIVERSITY PRESS

Great Clarendon Street, Oxford, OX2 6DP,
United Kingdom

Oxford University Press is a department of the University of Oxford.
It furthers the University's objective of excellence in research, scholarship,
and education by publishing worldwide. Oxford is a registered trade mark of
Oxford University Press in the UK and in certain other countries

Published in the United States of America by Oxford University Press
198 Madison Avenue, New York, NY 10016, United States of America

British Library Cataloguing in Publication Data
Data available

Library of Congress Control Number: 2017942397

ISBN 978-0-19-879100-3

Printed in Great Britain by
Ashford Colour Press Ltd, Gosport, Hampshire

For Kiran

Contents

Acknowledgements

I shall always be very grateful to the late Richard Gregory for introducing me to the delights of visual perception while I was a first-year undergraduate student and for his inspiration and friendship over the following years. My graduate supervisor and subsequent close friend, Stuart Anstis, showed me how to do (and how not to do) experiments as well as being a source of constant encouragement. The late Ian Howard showed me how to write more clearly and concisely and we shared an interest in building experimental apparatus to investigate perception in more real-world situations. I am also grateful to the many other colleagues and friends who have influenced the way I think about perception including Alan Cowey, Jan Koenderink, Christopher Tyler, Barbara Gillam, Alan Gilchrist, Bill Epstein, and my post-docs and students.

List of illustrations

Chapter 1
What is perception?

Definitions

What is perception? The word itself can be used in two different ways. First, it can refer to our *experience* of seeing, hearing, touching, tasting, and smelling objects and individuals in the surrounding world. As human observers, we are able to describe our subjective experiences—I see the sky as blue, I see my desk as having a particular size and shape, and I feel the texture of my sweater. Seeing is the particular word used to describe our visual experiences in contrast to our auditory, tactile, olfactory, and gustatory experiences. However, the word perception can also be used to refer to the *processes* that allow us to extract information from the patterns of energy that impinge on our sense organs. Thinking about perception as a set of processes has the advantage that it includes situations where there is no subjective experience—such as the control of our balance using visual and proprioceptive (felt position) information. In these cases, the information reaching our senses guides and controls our behaviour but there is no accompanying subjective experience. For the remainder of the book, I will use the word perception in this more general sense to refer to the use of sensory information whether or not it creates a subjective experience.

Some writers, such as the 19th-century scientist Hermann von Helmholtz, have suggested that there is a distinction between *sensations* and *perceptions*. He considered sensations to be the result of early or 'low-level' sensory processes in contrast to our perceptions that are thought to be a consequence of 'higher-level' processes that give sensations their meaning. However, this distinction raises awkward questions: first, is it possible to experience raw sensations that lack meaning? And second, how are we able to access the outputs of these low-level processes? A further assumption in the perception literature is that the processes responsible for our perceptions are not at all obvious or straightforward. For example, on the first page of Richard Gregory's excellent book *Eye and Brain*, he writes:

> We are so familiar with seeing, that it takes a leap of imagination to realise that there are problems to be solved. But consider it. We are given tiny distorted images in the eyes, and we see separate objects in surrounding space. From the patterns of stimulation on the retinas we perceive the world of objects, and this is nothing short of a miracle.

In Chapter 2, I am going to take issue with this characterization but for the moment we can see how this view is consistent with the fact that our perceptual systems can be fooled—we sometimes perceive the world incorrectly and experience illusions. One of the best-known examples is the Ames Room, named after its American inventor Adelbert Ames (Figure 1). Unlike most of the rooms we encounter, the Ames Room is not rectangular in shape but instead is trapezoidal with the far left corner much further away from the observer. However, when the room is viewed through a peephole using just one eye, it is seen as a normal rectangular room. Moreover, the two individuals standing in the two corners appear to be of very different sizes. There is a discrepancy between the reality—a trapezoidal-shaped room—and what we see—a normal, rectangular room—and hence our perception is labelled as illusory or non-veridical.

1. The Ames Room is trapezoidal in shape but from the particular peephole from which this photo was taken, the room is seen as a normal, rectangular room.

More recently, a similar theme of the difficulties faced by our perceptual systems has been highlighted by those working in the field of artificial intelligence and computational vision in their attempts to model our perceptual processes. In the visual modality, this is referred to as the problem of *inverse optics*. Conventional optics provides us with a description of how the patterns of light from the surrounding 3-D world reach the eye and create a 2-D image across the array of receptors we call the retina. In contrast, inverse optics—how we go from the 2-D retinal image to the 3-D world out there—is seen as problematic because there are many different 3-D scenes in the world that could have created exactly the same 2-D image (Figure 2). As a result, it is not obvious which of the possible real-world scenes was responsible for creating the image. Note that inverse optics is not just a problem for our perception of the 3-D world—similar problems exist in the perception of colour, motion, and form, as we shall see later.

3

2. The ambiguity of the retinal image illustrated in Magritte's painting *The Human Condition*. The real-world 3-D scene and the 2-D painting on the canvas create the same pattern of light at the eye.

Approaches to understanding perception

A theme that is common to both the traditional approaches to perception and the more recent computational research is that there is insufficient information in the patterns of light reaching the eyes (and similarly for the other senses) to explain the richness

3. A photo of a hollow (concave) mask of Beethoven but we perceive it to be a normal (convex) face.

and the lack of ambiguity in what we perceive. For many, the solution to this problem lies in our past experience and our knowledge of the world. Experience tells us that rooms are typically rectangular, rather than trapezoidal, and that faces are typically convex rather than concave. Hence, when we are faced with a trapezoidal room (Figure 1) or a hollow face (Figure 3), we choose the more likely interpretation based on our past experience. For the computational researchers, the solution to the ambiguity of the 2-D image is expressed in terms of the *constraints* that are incorporated into the processing mechanisms.

The alternative view, due largely to the work of the American psychologist James Gibson, is that there is actually a wealth of information in the patterns of energy reaching our senses and that the task for any perceptual system is to extract that information. As a consequence, there is no need to invoke ideas of inference or hypothesis testing. The difference between these two radically different conceptions of our perceptual processes is a theme that will recur throughout the book and you may find it remarkable that there is still no real consensus as to which of these approaches to the subject is the more appropriate. In writing this book, my intention is to de-mystify the process of perceiving by showing that there is, in reality, plenty of information to specify not just the low-level aspects of our perception—such as the lightness, colour, motion, depth, and form of objects in the surrounding world—but also their affordances (the significance of the information) for us as perceivers.

Chapter 2
Perceptual theories—direct, indirect, and computational

Background

The idea that the information reaching our senses is insufficient to account for the richness of our perceptions can be traced back to the writings of Hermann von Helmholtz in the 19th century. He thought of perception as a process of making 'unconscious inferences' about what is out there in the world. More recently, Richard Gregory has argued that our perceptions are like hypotheses in science—we make guesses about what is there in the surrounding world that are based on information from our knowledge and past experience. A variant on the same theme has been suggested by the American psychologist, Irvin Rock, who thought of our perceptions as being the result of 'intelligent, thought-like processes'. All three proposals are referred to as *indirect* or *constructivist* theories of perception and they share the idea that we need to construct or reconstruct our perceptions from limited sensory information. This view of perception sounds very plausible because we, as humans, are able to make *cognitive* inferences and hypotheses that go beyond the available evidence. Moreover, if our perceptions are only guesses or inferences about the external world, we should expect that we will sometimes perceive the world incorrectly and suffer from illusions, and this seems to be the case.

There is, however, a very different conception of our perceptual processes that was first suggested by the American psychologist James Gibson. He argued that far from being insufficient, the information reaching our senses is actually rich and, as a consequence, there is no need for elaboration or construction by processes such as inference or hypothesis testing. In his view, perceptual information merely needs to be 'picked up'. Moreover, he regarded the ambiguous and illusory situations that are used by the indirect theorists to support their theoretical position to be a consequence of the impoverished stimulus situations that are typical of many traditional experiments on perception. He pointed out that in the majority of those experiments, observers have to remain stationary and are obliged to keep their eyes fixed on a particular point in an unchanging scene. He contrasted this with everyday life where we are constantly moving around and gazing in different directions. Under these circumstances, our movements through the world create a constantly changing pattern of light at the eye(s) that he called *optic flow*. Optic flow not only provides information about the 3-D structure and layout of the world (exterospecific information) but also information about the observer's movements with respect to the world (propriospecific information).

This alternative theory of perception, which is usually referred to as *direct* perception, not only differs from indirect theories in the assumption that there is a sufficiency of information but also in terms of its conception of what perception is for. Traditional indirect theories have assumed that the primary purpose of perception is to create our subjective experiences—our *qualia* as the philosophers describe them. In contrast, Gibson claimed that the primary role of perceptual processes was to guide action and he had very little to say about subjective experience.

> Perceiving is an achievement of the individual, not an appearance in the theatre of his consciousness.

8

In this respect, Gibson can be thought to have more in common with the computational researchers like David Marr since it is clear that there is no place, and indeed no need, for subjective experience in a machine vision system. The idea of direct perception can also be thought to be more consistent with what we know about the perceptual systems of animals lower down on the phylogenetic scale. Their behaviour appears to be controlled more directly by the available sensory information and there appears to be no need to invoke ideas of inference or hypothesis testing, either consciously or unconsciously.

In his book *Vision*, David Marr argued that his view of perception had much in common with that of James Gibson. He wrote: 'In perception, perhaps the nearest anyone came to the level of computational theory was Gibson.' However, Marr went on to say that 'although some aspects of his thinking were along the right lines, he did not understand properly what information was, which led him to seriously underestimate the complexity of the information-processing problems involved in vision...'. Two questions arise. First, is it appropriate to characterize perception as an 'information processing task', and second, what does it mean to say that the information-processing problems of vision are 'complex'? Attempts to build machine vision systems to do basic perceptual tasks have proved to be extremely difficult but in what sense are the perceptual mechanisms of biological systems 'complex'? I will revisit the idea of complexity in Chapter 6.

Indirect or constructivist theories of perception

Let us consider these three different conceptions of what it means to perceive—the indirect, the direct, and the computational—in more detail. The origins of indirect or constructivist theory can be traced back to the physicist, physiologist, and vision scientist Hermann von Helmholtz who emphasized the importance of experience in shaping our perceptual abilities. His ideas can be contrasted with the nativist views of his rival Ewald Hering who believed in the importance of innate mechanisms in perception. The two are best known for their differing ideas of how we perceive colour—Helmholtz arguing for a trichromatic theory and Hering arguing for the involvement of opponent processes (see Chapter 3). However, their disagreement about the role of learning versus innate mechanisms is best illustrated in their contrasting views of how *visual direction* (the direction of objects with respect to the eye) might be coded. Simple geometry shows how the light coming from different points in space with respect to the eye is focused on different regions of the retina (Figure 4). As a consequence, there is a systematic relationship between the position of a point in space (with respect to the eye) and the location of its image on the retina. Both Helmholtz and Hering assumed that different receptors in the retina have different and unique *local signs*, that is, different receptors are tagged or labelled with a particular visual direction with respect to the eye. They differed, however, in their views of how those retinal receptors acquire their local signs. Hering believed that local signs were innately given whereas Helmholtz argued that they needed to be learned (calibrated). Helmholtz suggested that the information used to calibrate the local signs comes from the magnitude and direction of the eye movements needed to bring the image of a particular peripheral point in space onto the fovea. As an aside, it is interesting to note that in spite of Helmholtz's strong empiricist views, his theory assumes that some things must be innate. In particular, (i) that eye movement signals are given (i.e. they do not need to be learned) and (ii) that the fovea of the retina has a special status in that its local sign is innately given. Helmholtz's suggestion that local signs need to be calibrated is, of course, consistent with the philosopher George Berkeley's idea that 'touch educates vision'.

Helmholtz's empiricist view of perception was accompanied by a belief that what we perceive goes beyond what is available to the senses. Insufficiency of information is the essence of constructivist theory. He argued that our perceptions are based on a process of

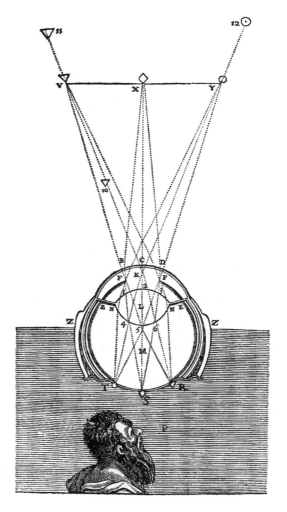

4. The projection of light rays onto the retinal surface of the eye illustrated in René Descartes's *La Dioptrique*. There is a one-to-one relationship between the location of a point with respect to the eye (e.g. point 12) and the location of its image on the retina (T).

'unconscious inference' whereby we seek meaningful explanations of the patterns of stimulation reaching our senses. In his *Handbook of Physiological Optics* he wrote:

> The sensations of the senses are tokens for consciousness, it being
> left to our intelligence to learn how to comprehend their meaning…

More recently, Richard Gregory put forward a similar idea in his proposal that we use induction to create 'perceptual hypotheses' from the data obtained from the senses. Gregory drew a parallel with the way in which we make hypotheses in science that go beyond the limited empirical data. In other words, both Helmholtz and Gregory share the assumption that perception is an inferential process with the need to make guesses (inferences or hypotheses) about what the sensory information means. In his book *The Logic of Perception*, Irvin Rock suggested that our perceptions are the result of 'intelligent thought-like processes'. All three indirect theories make similar assumptions: (i) perception is a process of construction rather than the result of some direct, mechanistic process; (ii) the information reaching our senses is insufficient to account for the richness of what we perceive; (iii) meaning is added rather than contained in the sense data.

These ideas seem eminently plausible because we, as humans, are clearly able to make inferences and hypotheses at a conscious, cognitive level that go beyond the available evidence. Rock contrasted his idea of indirect perception—in which there is no simple, one-to-one relationship between sense data and what we perceive—with Gibson's idea of direct perception, which Rock characterized as a 'stimulus theory'. In animal learning, we know that particular stimuli trigger particular responses and Rock argued that Gibson's direct theory implies that there is a direct link between stimuli and our perceptions (S → P). To refute this idea, Rock pointed out that there are many situations where a single stimulus can give rise to multiple percepts, using examples of ambiguous figures like the Necker cube and Rubin's vase

(a) (b)

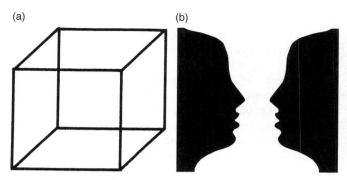

5. The ambiguous Necker cube and the ambiguous Rubin's vase figure show that the same 'stimulus' can give rise to two or more percepts.

(Figure 5). The logic is that perception cannot be direct because the same stimulus can give rise to two or more percepts. Moreover, the evidence of ambiguous figures suggests that the visual system has to make choices. In his description of the Necker cube, Richard Gregory argues that the visual system 'entertains alternative hypotheses'.

There are also cases where multiple stimuli can result in the same percept which, once again, would not be expected if there were a simple, one-to-one link between stimuli and percepts. For example, the same object viewed at different distances creates differently sized images on the retina but we typically perceive the object as having roughly the same physical size. This process is referred to as size constancy and similar examples can be found in shape, lightness, colour, and depth constancy. Rock's explanation of these constancy effects is that other information is 'taken into account'—information about distance for size constancy; information about surface orientation for shape constancy; information about illumination level for lightness constancy, and so on. There is a third class of perceptual effects that provides evidence against direct perception—illusions. Illusions, as we shall see in Chapter 7, are typically defined as situations where there is a mismatch between the physical reality and what we perceive. If we experience illusions, this shows that there cannot be any direct link between the stimulus (physical reality) and what we perceive.

In summary, the key idea of indirect theory is that perception is a constructive process that involves inference, learning, and past experience. As a consequence, illusions are readily accounted for because there is no direct link between a stimulus and what we perceive. It is also assumed that meaning is added (rather than contained in the pattern of stimulation) and that perception should be seen as an achievement of the perceiver. These ideas can be summed up in the pun—'There is more to perception than meets the eye.'

Direct theories of perception

The idea of direct perception owes much to the work of the American psychologist James Gibson and it is instructive to see how his ideas changed between his first book *The Perception of the Visual World*, published in 1950, and his last book *The Ecological Approach to Visual Perception*, published in 1979. Gibson's initial intention was to challenge the prevailing assumption of the indirect theorists that the information in the sensory input was inadequate to explain the richness of our perceptions. For example, he pointed out that the world we inhabit is typically made up of surfaces rather than isolated points and lines and that the texture elements that cover these surfaces create gradients of size at the retina. Moreover, the same textured surfaces create gradients of disparity between the two eyes and gradients of motion when we move (Figures 6(a) and 6(b)). These gradients are a simple consequence of the projective geometry of the surrounding world but their significance lies in the rich information they provide about the spatial layout of the world.

Gibson's second important insight was that we are constantly moving around in the world. Our movements create a changing,

6. (a) Gradients of size, density, and foreshortening created by a cobbled surface. (b) Gradients of motion created when the observer walks down a long corridor.

transforming image on the retina and the transforming image contains information about the 3-D layout of the surrounding world as well as information about our own movements within that world. This approach contrasts with the way in which the majority of experiments on perception are carried out where observers are asked to view a single, static picture, often for just a very brief period of time. Moreover, observers are often asked to maintain fixation on a particular point in the static scene. The usual justification for demanding fixation is that it avoids a possible confound from eye movements but it also prevents the observer from using the information that is available in normal, active vision. In other words, remaining stationary and fixating 'throws the baby out with the bathwater'.

In the 1950s, both these ideas were novel but nowadays no one would disagree with the importance of texture gradients and optic flow, whatever his or her theoretical views. Gibson put forward a much more radical idea in his second book: *The Senses Considered as Perpetual Systems*, published in 1968. In that book, he rejected the idea of the *stimulus* as the appropriate description of the input to our perceptual systems. Gibson argued that stimuli excite the sensory receptors (in the eye, ear, skin, nose, and mouth) but that *information* excites what he called the *perceptual system*. Information is contained (or may be present) in the spatio-temporal patterns of light that reach the eye—it is not the light itself. In audition, information about the meaning of an utterance is contained in the temporal patterns of sound energy reaching the ear—it is not the air pressure changes themselves. Apart from anything else, this makes the problem of how we integrate information from the different senses more tractable. Different energies excite different sorts of receptors in the different sensory modalities but the information they provide is 'of the same sort'. It is important to point out that Gibson's concept of information is quite different from the idea of information as 'knowledge communicated to a receiver' that can be specified mathematically, as in Shannon and Weaver's mathematical theory of communication. For Gibson, information refers to the 'specification of the observer's environment'.

In his last book, Gibson claimed that 'The retinal image is not necessary for vision', which may have given many readers the impression that we do not need eyes in order to see! What he meant was that the retinal image is not the appropriate starting point for trying to understand the processes of perception and can be misleading for several reasons. It is misleading because the majority of seeing creatures do not have chambered eyes (like ours) in which there is a lens to focus an image on an array of receptors (Figure 4). More subtly, it is misleading because there is a hidden implication that something is looking at the retinal image. Gibson wrote: 'we (mistakenly) think of the image as *something to be seen*'. Note that philosophers have long rejected the so-called problem of the inverted retinal image as a non-problem on the grounds that there is nothing 'looking at' the inverted image. However, Gibson was not the first to suggest that emphasizing the characteristics of the retinal image can be misleading. A similar view was expressed 150 years ago by Helmholtz when he wrote:

> I am myself disposed to think that neither the size, form and position of the real retina nor the distortions of the image projected on it matter at all, as long as the image is sharply delineated all over... In the natural consciousness of the spectator the retina has no existence whatever.

If the retinal image is not the appropriate starting point for trying to understand perception, what is? This is where Gibson introduced the concept of the *optic array*—a description of how light is structured at a particular vantage point (Figure 7(a)). The optic array is a description, in angular terms, of the light reflected off the multitude of objects that surround us in the world. It is structured in the sense that smaller features like the leaves on a tree are nested within the larger structure of the tree which, in turn, is nested within the environmental layout. Why did Gibson choose to talk about the optic array rather than the retinal image, given that the retinal image is merely the projection of the optic array onto the retina? The answer is twofold. First, not all seeing creatures have chambered eyes, in which an image is projected by a lens onto a retinal surface, and second, by talking about the optic array it allows us to separate out the question of whether or not there is information from whether or not a particular animal can use that information. Take binocular, stereoscopic vision as an example. Many writers talk about the 3-D information that is contained in the small differences or disparities between the two retinal images but those differences arise because we have two spatially separated eyes that provide us with two different *vantage points* from which to view the world. In other words, the information about the 3-D structure of the world exists independently of the particular characteristics of the visual system used to view the world.

Gibson extended the optic array concept to consider the information contained in the transforming optic array as the observer (or, strictly speaking, the vantage point) moves (Figure 7(b)). He provided examples of how the available information could, in principle, tell us about both the structure of the surrounding world and the characteristics of our own movements within it. Traditionally, perception has been thought of as a one-way process in which our perception of the world allows us to move around but, as Gibson pointed out, we also move around in order to perceive. Gibson also proposed a quite different way of thinking about the underlying processes and mechanisms of perception. He rejected the idea of 'information processing' and argued instead that a more appropriate model was that of 'information pick-up'. He proposed that the perceptual system should be thought of as a system that 'resonates' to the spatio-temporal patterns of energy reaching our senses in a similar way to a tuned electronic circuit that resonates to radio waves of a particular frequency. Moreover, his conception of the role of

(a)

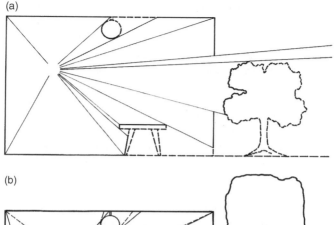

(b)

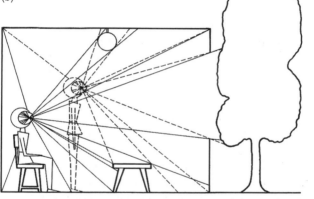

7. (a) Gibson's ambient optic array and (b) the transforming optic array when the observer and vantage point move.

learning in perception was not one of laying down memories that subsequently affect what we perceive but rather of a perceptual system that becomes *attuned* through experience. Some of Gibson's critics have argued that he put too much emphasis on innate mechanisms but, in reality, perceptual learning plays an equally important role in his idea of direct perception, as is evident from the developmental studies carried out by his wife Eleanor.

One of the reasons why traditional theorists have assumed that perception is difficult or complicated is that the input to the sensory systems is constantly changing—the retinal size of an object changes with changes in the object's distance from the observer, the retinal shape of an object changes with its orientation with respect to the observer, the amount of light reflected from a particular surface changes with the changes in the illumination, and the composition of the light reflected from a particular surface changes with the spectral composition of the illumination. Gibson's answer to these so-called problems is that we should consider the things that stay the same—the so-called *invariant* properties of the stimulation—rather than emphasizing the things that change. The relative sizes of different objects in a scene remain the same with changes of viewing distance; the relative shapes of different objects remain the same with changes of viewing angle; the relative amounts of light reflected from different surfaces remain the same with changes in the intensity of the illumination; and the relative spectral compositions of the light reflected from different surfaces remain the same with changes in the spectral composition of the illumination.

The final step in the development of Gibson's theory was to reject the assumption that the purpose of perception was object identification and recognition. In most traditional theories of perception, the attachment of 'meaning' is seen as a stage that comes after object recognition (cf. David Marr's theory of vision), but for Gibson, 'meaning' is the very essence of perception—it is what perception is for. But Gibson never used the word 'meaning', because that word has the connotation of some higher-level, cognitive process of 'knowing'. Instead, he talked about *affordances*—which he defined as 'what the world offers us'. A tree stump affords 'sitting-on'—at least to us as humans—and a particular surface affords 'walking-on'. In other words, meaning is not something that is added on afterwards but is the reason why we have evolved perceptual systems in the first place.

In summary, the first and most important idea of direct theory is that perception is a process of information pick-up that does not depend on processes of construction, enrichment, or embellishment. Second, gradients and optic flow provide examples of the richness of the available information. Third, information rather than stimulation is the correct starting point for understanding perception, and fourth, sensory processes should not be thought of in isolation but instead as part of an overall perceptual system. Fifth, perception is best understood as a synergy or mutuality between the perceiver and the environment.

Computational theories of perception

Since the 1960s, there have been many attempts to model the perceptual processes using computer algorithms, and the most influential figure of the last forty years has been David Marr, working at MIT. His book *Vision: A Computational Investigation into Human Representation and Processing of Visual Information* was published shortly after his untimely death in 1980. He started the book with his own definition of seeing:

> the process of discovering from images what is present in the world and where it is.

and he went on to say:

> Vision is therefore, first and foremost, an information processing task...

Marr and his colleagues were responsible for developing detailed algorithms for extracting (i) low-level information about the location of contours in the visual image, (ii) the motion of those contours, and (iii) the 3-D structure of objects in the world from binocular disparities and optic flow. In addition, one of his lasting achievements was to encourage researchers to be more rigorous in the way that perceptual tasks are described, analysed, and formulated and to use computer models to test the predictions of those models against human performance.

Before considering the particular perceptual tasks that Marr attempted to model, it is useful to consider his underlying assumptions. First, Marr asserted that vision is an 'information processing problem'. What does this mean? For Marr, information processing is intimately linked with the idea of *representation* which he defines as 'a formal system for making *explicit* certain entities or types of information'. John Frisby has described representations as 'symbolic descriptions'. Marr used the example of the different ways in which numbers can be represented, for example, using the Arabic, Roman, or binary number systems. As a consequence, the algorithms (procedures) used to add or subtract numbers are quite different and they depend on the way in which numbers are represented. The terms *representation* and *algorithm* are derived from computing and it makes sense to describe the operation of a computer using these terms. The problem, as I see it, is whether such terms are meaningful for describing a biological system such as the human perceptual system. Are there algorithms and representations in the brain and is there any need to make something 'explicit'? If the terms are used in an 'as if' sense—that is, we might think about perceptual processing 'as if' there are algorithms and representations in the brain—I would be less concerned but there are many who would like to believe in the reality of algorithms and representations in the brain. I prefer to think of the computational approach in the 'as if' sense—as being a powerful way of modelling the perceptual system that can be contrasted with the inadequate hydraulic and telephone exchange models that have been proposed in the past. Geoffrey Hinton has written:

> computer programs have provided an information-processing metaphor in which computation is performed by the sequential application of explicit stored rules to explicit symbolic expressions.

It is quite a good metaphor for what happens when people do arithmetic computations, but perception isn't like that.

Marr's other main assumption was that any information processing system can be understood at a number of different levels: (i) the computational theory level, (ii) the algorithmic level, and (iii) the level of mechanism. The computational theory level is the level at which 'the goal of the computation' is identified and 'the logic of the strategy by which it can be carried out'. In the representation or algorithmic level, the algorithms for transforming the chosen representations are identified. The physical realization of both algorithm and representation takes place at the level of mechanism—the hardware implementation. Marr emphasized the relative independence of these three levels of explanation and argued that it might not be possible to infer what is happening at a different level from the one being investigated. For example, even though we know a great deal about the nature of colour constancy from behavioural and psychophysical evidence, this does not tell us how the process might be implemented at a physiological or mechanism level. Likewise, the discovery of cells in the visual cortex that have spatially and chromatically opponent receptive fields is important but it does not tell us how colour constancy is achieved (see Chapters 3 and 7).

For Marr, the most important of the three levels is that of the computational theory—setting out what the visual system is trying to achieve—and he rightly criticizes the tendency of visual psychophysicists to investigate striking effects without thinking about why we have perceptual systems in the first place. My favourite example to illustrate this point comes from the wealth of papers that appeared after Celeste McCullough's discovery of colour contingent after-effects in the 1960s. She reported that if you ask an observer to view an alternating display (every five seconds) of a red and black vertical grating pattern and a green and black horizontal grating pattern for ten minutes, a subsequently presented black and white vertical grating pattern appears slightly greenish and a subsequently presented black and white horizontal grating pattern appears slightly pinkish. In other words, the colour of the after-effect is contingent on the orientation of the black and white test pattern. The other remarkable characteristic of these contingent after-effects is that they can last for several days or even weeks. McCullough's discovery resulted in a plethora of papers reporting a range of other contingent after-effects but there was rather little discussion of what those effects might mean or whether they have any real significance for our understanding of the human visual system.

Given that Marr argued that the computational theory level was the most important of the three levels of explanation, it is appropriate to ask what he considered to be the principal computational goal of early visual processing. The answer is object recognition—'what is present in the world and where it is'. The hierarchical stages of Marr's model of early visual processing culminate in what he referred to as the '3-D model' representation where the viewer-independent 3-D structure of an object is made explicit using volumetric primitives (Figure 8). Marr was keen to stress that the attachment of meaning only comes after these 'rich symbolic descriptions' have been created by the early processing mechanisms.

Over the past fifteen years, many researchers in the field of perception have characterized perception as a Bayesian process, named after its originator—the Reverend Thomas Bayes in the 18th century. Bayes' rule states that the probability of perceiving a particular state of the world, given a particular sensory input: p(state|sensory input) is the product of the probability of that particular sensory input given that state of the world: p(sensory input|state) and the a priori probability of that particular state: p(state). The crucial term here is the a priori probability of the particular state: p(state)—which is referred to as the *prior*.

Take, for example, the observation that the shading pattern in Figure 9(a) is seen as a series of (concave) craters or hollows. Why

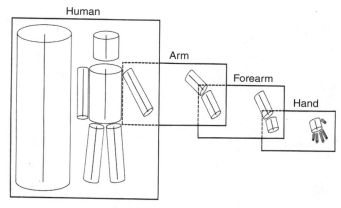

8. The volumetric primitives (elongated cylinders) that Marr thought could be used to describe and identify different objects.

should this be the case given that a similar pattern of light and dark could also be created by a series of (convex) bumps or mounds (Figure 9(b))? The particular shading pattern is essentially ambiguous—it could correspond to craters lit from above or bumps lit from below and therefore the probability of this particular sensory input given this state is 0.5. However, if we assume that there is a *prior* in our visual system that light usually comes from above, this will bias our perception so that the pattern of light and dark in Figure 9(a) is seen as a series of craters and the same pattern of light and dark (but rotated through 180 degrees) is seen as a series of mounds.

According to Bayesian theory, what we perceive is a consequence of probabilistic processes that depend on the likelihood of certain events occurring in the particular world we live in. Moreover, most Bayesian models of perceptual processes assume that there is noise in the sensory signals and the amount of noise affects the reliability of those signals—the more noise, the less reliable the signal. Over the past fifteen years, Bayes theory has been used

(a)   (b)

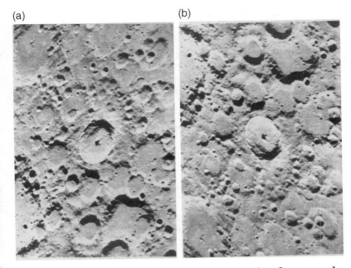

9. The shading pattern on the left (a) is seen as a series of craters and the shading pattern on the right (b) is seen as a series of mounds. In fact, (b) is just a 180-degree rotated version of (a). If the visual system makes the assumption—has the *prior*—that light comes from above, the surface on the left should be seen as craters and the surface on the right as mounds.

extensively to model the interaction between different discrepant cues, such as binocular disparity and texture gradients to specify the slant of an inclined surface. We will come across Bayes theory again in connection with experiments on 3-D vision.

Evidence from neurophysiology and anatomy

The last fifty years have seen a massive growth in our knowledge and understanding of the neurophysiology and anatomy of the perceptual systems based on evidence from single cell recordings, evoked potentials, and brain scanning. How this evidence fits with these different conceptual frameworks will be discussed in Chapter 8.

Summary

Each of the three theoretical positions described so far has attempted to define what perception *is* as well as making suggestions as to how perception might be achieved—the processes involved. The constructivists' aim has been to account for what we see—our subjective experience of the world—and how this is achieved using inferential processes because the sensory input is insufficient. The aim of the direct theorists, on the other hand, has been to account for the way our actions in the world are guided and controlled by the assumed richness of the information picked up by our perceptual systems. For most computational theorists, the goal of perception is assumed to be the identification of objects in the surrounding world by exploiting the constraints of that world. An important consequence of these different theoretical positions is that different researchers have typically chosen to investigate rather different aspects of this thing we call perception. The constructivists have concentrated on trying to understand our perceptual processes using the evidence from situations where the perceptual system makes mistakes. In contrast, the direct theorists have typically chosen situations where the perceptual systems provide correct answers—for instance, where there is a clear link between the information available in the spatio-temporal patterning of light reaching the eye(s) and the control of our actions. The computational theorists, on the other hand, have sought to provide a much more rigorous structure for understanding the tasks of early visual processing using mathematics and modelling.

In Chapters 3–8 my approach will be to try to understand our perceptual systems as the consequence of evolutionary pressures that have allowed us and other species to survive within the particular ecological niches we inhabit. This approach assumes, and I will attempt to demonstrate, that there is indeed rich information in spatio-temporal patterns of energy that reach the senses not only to specify the physical characteristics of the surrounding world but also to specify their 'meaning' for the animal. From now on, the word 'information' will be used in the sense of being a 'specification of the observer's environment'. The emphasis will be on visual perception because vision is our most important sense but similar ideas and examples can be found in each of the sensory modalities.

Chapter 3
Lightness and colour

The evolution of our perceptual systems has depended on the successful pick-up of perceptual information that is vital for survival. It follows that the information has to be meaningful for a particular species. A tree stump has a very different 'meaning' for a human who is looking for a place to sit compared to an insect seeking a nest-site. The pattern of light reflected from the tree stump is the same in both cases but the information it provides is quite different for different species. Information is *species-specific*. But how do we know what the information is? If you think about it, there must be information in the spatio-temporal patterns of energy reaching our senses because humans and insects respond appropriately but this does not tell us what the information might be. The indirect theorists argue that the sensory information is insufficient and has to be supplemented by past experience and our knowledge of the world. However, it seems to me that this is the same as saying that we have a beautifully attuned perceptual system that has been modified by, and has benefited from, both evolution and a lifetime of experience. For present purposes, it is less important whether we, or the members of another species, have to learn the meaning (the affordance) of a particular spatio-temporal pattern of energy or whether that ability is based on innate mechanisms. In both cases, there has to be something in the pattern of energy that contains the required information. In this chapter, I will concentrate on visual perception and I will try to identify some of the characteristics of the patterns of light reaching our eyes that might contribute to the information we need for survival. However, it is important to stress that the pick-up of particular perceptual characteristics—the lightness and colour of the surfaces that surround us—should not be thought of as ends in themselves but rather as a contribution to a perceptual system that has evolved to allow us to act successfully in a particular ecological niche.

Lightness perception

All surfaces have the property of reflectance—that is, the extent to which they reflect (rather than absorb) the incident illumination—and those reflectances can vary between 0 per cent and 100 per cent. Surfaces can also be selective in the particular wavelengths they reflect or absorb. Our colour vision depends on these selective reflectance properties, as we shall see in the section 'Colour perception'. Reflectance characteristics describe the physical properties of surfaces. The *lightness* of a surface refers to a perceptual judgement of a surface's reflectance characteristic—whether it appears as black or white or some grey level in between. Note that we are talking about the perception of *lightness*—rather than brightness—which refers to our estimate of how much light is coming from a particular surface or is emitted by a source of illumination. The perception of surface lightness is one of the most fundamental perceptual abilities because it allows us not only to differentiate one surface from another but also to identify the real-world properties of a particular surface.

Many textbooks start with the observation that lightness perception is a difficult task because the amount of light reflected from a particular surface depends on both the reflectance characteristic of the surface and the intensity of the incident illumination. For example, a piece of black paper under high illumination will reflect back more light to the eye than a piece of white paper under dim illumination. As a consequence, lightness constancy—the ability to correctly judge the lightness of a surface under different illumination conditions—is often considered to be an 'achievement' of the perceptual system. As with other so-called constancies, it is argued that we have to 'take into account' other information—in this case, information about the intensity of the illumination. Hence, if we 'knew' something about the intensity of the illumination, we would be able to correct for, or discount, the consequences of the illumination. The mistake in thinking about the issue in this way is that it assumes that something needs to be corrected in order to achieve lightness constancy.

The invariants of lightness perception

The alternative starting point for understanding lightness perception is to ask whether there is something that remains constant or invariant in the patterns of light reaching the eye with changes of illumination. In this case, it is the relative amount of light reflected off different surfaces. Consider two surfaces that have different reflectances—two shades of grey. The actual amount of light reflected off each of the surfaces will vary with changes in the illumination but the relative amount of light reflected off the two surfaces remains the same. This shows that lightness perception is necessarily a spatial task and hence a task that cannot be solved by considering one particular surface alone. Note that the relative amount of light reflected off different surfaces does not tell us about the absolute lightnesses of different surfaces—only their relative lightnesses—a point I shall return to in this section. However, in order to use the information provided by the relative amounts of reflected light we need to 'assume' that the light illuminating the different surfaces is the same—that is, spatially homogeneous or only slowly changing over space. (The use of the word 'assume' carries no implication of some higher-level process of 'assuming'. It is simply a statement about the way the visual system has evolved and how it is wired up.) If we inhabited a world in which the only sources of illumination were spotlights that illuminated just a small part of the visual world (e.g. my shirt), measurements of the relative amount of light reflected from my shirt would be an unreliable indicator of my shirt's lightness. However, most light sources in the world in which we have evolved (including the sun and the sky) provide relatively even illumination to different surfaces, at least over localized regions of space. Indirect illumination and the shadows cast by other objects complicate the situation but it should not surprise us that our visual system has evolved to deal with these complications. Alan Gilchrist has proposed that the visual system makes the appropriate spatial comparisons within different 'frames of reference' (Figure 10) and that the highest luminance in the scene is used to determine or 'anchor' the lightnesses of all other parts of the scene. He has also shown that the anchoring process is neither entirely local nor entirely global but instead depends on the size and degree of *articulation* (the complexity of the surroundings) within a particular framework.

Can our perception of lightness be fooled? Yes, of course it can and the ways in which we make mistakes in our perception of the lightnesses of surfaces can tell us much about the characteristics of the underlying processes. However, there are some demonstrations of the failures of lightness perception that, in my view, tell us very little. Take, for example, Ted Adelson's checker shadow illusion (Figure 11). The image depicts a cylindrical object resting on a checkerboard and casting a shadow over the light and dark squares of the checkerboard. A dark and a light square (marked A and B) are seen as dark grey and light grey respectively, but when the rest of the scene is masked off so that only the two particular squares are visible, they are seen to have the same grey colour. It is an illusion, some have claimed, because the two squares are seen as dark and light even though the amount of light from each square is the same. The mistake in coming to this conclusion is in thinking that the amount of light from a particular surface can tell us something about the lightness of the surface—it can't. Another way of making the same point is to imagine that

10. A photograph, based on figure 11.2 in Alan Gilchrist's book *Seeing Light and Dark*, showing how a series of superimposed patches with the same shade of grey can appear very different in different parts of the scene. We perceive lightness within local frames of reference such as the areas in shadow and the areas that receive direct illumination.

11. Adelson's checker shadow illusion. The amount of light reaching the eye is the same for patches A and B but A is seen as a dark square and B as a light square.

the checker shadow picture in Figure 11 is a real 3-D scene that we are viewing in the world. We would not regard the identification of one square as light and the other as dark as an illusion—it would be seen as a correct perception because square A is dark and square B is light! The fact that the picture was created artificially and probably doesn't correspond precisely to an actual real-world scene is irrelevant. What the demonstration actually shows is that our ability to correctly judge the lightnesses of surfaces works remarkable well, even when there are shadows in the scene.

So far, I have considered how our ability to perceive the lightnesses of surfaces correctly depends on making relative, spatial comparisons with neighbouring surfaces. However, the spatial pattern of light reflected from a particular surface can also provide information about the 3-D structure of that surface. For example, the amount of light reflected from the surface of the cylinder in Adelson's checker shadow illusion (Figure 11) varies and the spatial changes of the reflected light provide information about the object's cylindrical shape. This is referred to as shape-from-shading. That information is based on the physics of the situation: the amount of light reflected from a surface depends on its orientation to the incident illumination. The maximum amount of light is reflected when a surface is at right angles to the incident light and falls off according to the cosine of the angle of the surface. Shape-from-shading information is discussed in more detail in Chapter 5 on depth perception.

Colour perception

From a survival point of view, the ability to differentiate objects and surfaces in the world by their 'colours' (spectral reflectance characteristics) can be extremely useful—two surfaces that reflect the same *overall* amount of light to the eye can be distinguished by the way in which the two surfaces reflect particular wavelengths. Most species of mammals, birds, fish, and insects possess several different types of receptor, each of which has a different *spectral sensitivity function* (Figure 12). As we shall see, having two types of receptor with different spectral sensitivities is the minimum necessary for colour vision. This is referred to as dichromacy and the majority of mammals are dichromats with the exception of the old world monkeys and humans.

Colour is regarded by many philosophers as a secondary perceptual property on the grounds that colour—for example redness or blueness—does not exist in the world. We have an awareness of the redness or blueness of a surface as the result of our *qualia* (subjective experiences) and we can share those subjective experiences with other observers through the use of common language and labels. However, there is no way of telling whether

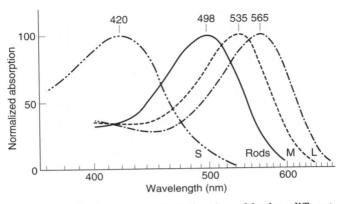

12. The normalized spectral sensitivity functions of the three different types of cone receptor (S, M, and L) and the rod receptors (solid line) in the human retina. Note that the sensitivity of each of the three cone types (and the rod receptors) extends over a wide range of wavelengths and hence they should not be regarded as 'red' or 'green' or 'blue' cones.

my subjective awareness of a red colour is the same as yours. This does not mean that there is no physical basis for our ability to discriminate and identify differently coloured objects. Different surfaces have different reflectance characteristics, as discussed previously for lightness perception. The only difference between lightness and colour perception is that in the latter case we have to consider the way a surface selectively reflects (and absorbs) different wavelengths, rather than just a surface's average reflectance over all wavelengths. Hence it is possible to design a machine vision system that is capable of extracting information about the selective reflectances of different surfaces (their 'colours') in a similar way to the human visual system. Moreover, that machine system could also have a similar ability to discriminate, 'identify', and give different labels to different coloured surfaces even though the machine system has no subjective experiences of those colours.

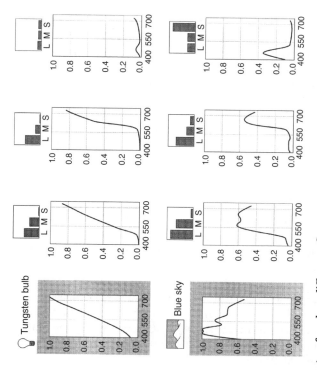

13. The three different surfaces have different reflectance properties but the wavelengths of light reflected from a given surface are also influenced by the spectral composition of the illumination — tungsten bulb (top row) or blue sky (bottom row). The responses of the three cone types (L, M, and S) are shown above the graphs.

The similarities between the tasks of extracting lightness and colour information mean that we can ask a similar question about colour perception—what is the invariant information that could specify the reflectance characteristic of a surface? Once again, it cannot be the intensities of the wavelengths reflected from a particular surface because these are affected by both the reflectance characteristic of the surface (its 'colour') and the spectral composition of the illuminating light (Figure 13). A sheet of white paper viewed under the yellow light of a sunset will reflect more medium wavelength light than a sheet of yellow paper under the blueish daylight. The information that is invariant under changes of spectral illumination is the relative amounts of long, medium, and short wavelength light reaching our eyes from different surfaces in the scene. Edwin Land and John McCann referred to these spatial patterns of relative reflectances under long, medium, and short wavelength light as *lightness records*.

Lightness records

Figure 14 shows three black and white photographs of the same coloured scene taken through red, green, and blue filters respectively. A red filter is one that selectively absorbs medium and short wavelengths and maximally transmits long wavelengths, whereas a green filter selectively absorbs long and short wavelengths and maximally transmits medium wavelengths. Hence it is likely that the light regions in the red lightness record of Figure 14 were produced by objects that reflected a significant amount of long wavelength ('red') light in the original scene. In Land and McCann's *retinex* model, the relative lightness of a given region in the red-filtered black and white photograph is compared with the relative lightness of the same region in the green- and blue-filtered black and white photographs. When the relative lightnesses of a given region are compared, they reveal that the region must have been 'reddish' in the original scene. Note that even if there is more long wavelength (red) light

14. The three lightness records of the same coloured scene. These black and white photographs were taken through red (upper left), green (upper right), and blue (lower) filters respectively. The white mushrooms show up as light in all three records whereas the yellow bananas are lightest in the red and green records. The green pepper in the upper right is lightest in the green record and the red pepper in the lower left is lightest in the red record.

illuminating the entire scene, this would affect all surfaces in the scene but would leave the the relative lightnesses of different regions of the scene relatively unaffected.

In order for this to be true, it is necessary to assume that the luminance and chromatic properties of the illumination are approximately the same (i.e. homogeneous) over the scene, or at least only slowly changing. As with lightness perception, this is true for most natural sources of illumination in our world. The task that faces vision scientists is to discover the precise details of the spatial comparisons that are made in the human visual system, and it seems likely that these will be made within similar 'frames of reference' to those proposed by Gilchrist for lightness perception. Answers to these questions require the behavioural evidence of our ability to judge colour surfaces correctly as well as the mistakes and errors we make under particular viewing conditions.

The preceding discussion makes it clear that the successful identification and discrimination of coloured surfaces is dependent on making spatial comparisons between the amounts of short, medium, and long wavelength light reaching our eyes from different surfaces. As with lightness perception, colour perception is necessarily a spatial task. It follows that if a scene is illuminated by the light of just a single wavelength, the appropriate spatial comparisons cannot be made. This can be demonstrated by illuminating a real-world scene containing many different coloured objects with yellow, sodium light that contains only a single wavelength. All objects, whatever their 'colours', will only reflect back to the eye different intensities of that sodium light and hence there will only be absolute but no relative differences between the short, medium, and long wavelength lightness records. There is a similar, but less dramatic, effect on our perception of colour when the spectral characteristics of the illumination are restricted to just a few wavelengths, as is the case with fluorescent lighting. The colours of clothes can look very different in a shop with fluorescent lighting compared with natural lighting that contains a wide range of wavelengths.

I have argued that the correct identification and perception of surface colour requires a visual system to make both spatial and chromatic comparisons but why did Land and McCann's retinex model involve making comparisons between three different lightness records? Why not two or four or some other number? Logically, it has to be true that just two lightness records of a coloured scene would be sufficient to un-confound the effects of illumination and surface colour. To convince you that this is the case, imagine taking just two black and white photographs through red and green filters respectively, thereby creating just two different lightness records. In this case, there is information about the 'colour' of different parts of the scene in the relative ratios of lightnesses between objects in the two lightness records and those ratios will be largely unaffected by changes in either the intensity of the illumination or its chromatic characteristics.

Land famously demonstrated the possibility of colour vision based on two channels (or receptor types) using just two lightness records. He did this by projecting and superimposing the images of two black and white slides (taken through red and green filters respectively) using red and green filters over the two projectors. We see a wide range of different colours. Even more dramatically, he showed that when the images of the same two black and white slides (taken through red and green filters respectively) are projected and superimposed on a screen with a red filter over one projector and *no* filter over the second projector, observers report seeing a range of colours even though each local area on the screen was illuminated by a mixture of just red and white light. This demonstration is important because it shows the necessity of making spatial comparisons for colour perception—if the rest of the scene is masked off, each individual region will be seen as either red or white or a shade of pink but when the visual system is able to make the spatial comparisons, we see a wide gamut of colours.

Trichromacy

The answer to the question of why Land and McCann's retinex model was based on three lightness records can be traced back to the observations made by Thomas Young and Hermann von Helmholtz in the 19th century. Although there was no physiological evidence to support his claim, Young proposed that human colour vision was based on just three different types of receptors. The key

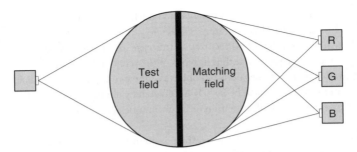

15. A split-screen matching field. The observer's task is to adjust the mixture of three different wavelengths (primaries) in the right-hand part of the field until the colour matches the test patch displayed in the left-hand part of the field.

evidence to support the idea of trichromacy is that the majority of colour shades can be matched by a suitable mixture of light from just three different light sources or 'primaries'. This can be demonstrated using a split screen display in which the coloured test patch to be matched is located in one half of the matching field and, in the other half, the observer is able to adjust the intensities of three different coloured lights (Figure 15). The three different coloured lights are typically red, green, and blue, that is, with their peak wavelengths in the long, medium, and short wavelength regions of the visible spectrum, although it turns out that many different 'primaries' (coloured lights) can be used. These matching experiments show that a white test patch can be matched with a roughly equal mixture of the three different coloured lights whereas a yellow test patch requires a mixture consisting predominantly of just long and medium wavelength light. The crucial finding is that matches cannot be achieved using just two different coloured light sources and observers do not require more than three light sources to obtain a good match. From this we can deduce that human colour vision is based on just three different types of receptors that are selectively sensitive to light in different parts of the visible spectrum—the trichromatic theory of colour vision (Figure 12).

Why do these matching experiments suggest that human colour vision is trichromatic? Consider a single receptor mechanism, such as a rod receptor in the human visual system, that responds to a limited range of wavelengths—referred to as the receptor's spectral sensitivity function (Figure 16(a)). This hypothetical receptor is more sensitive to some wavelengths (around 550 nm) than others and we might be tempted to think that a single type of receptor could provide information about the wavelength of the light reaching the receptor. This is not the case, however, because an increase or decrease in the response of that receptor could be due to either a change in the wavelength or an increase or decrease in the amount of light reaching the receptor. In other words, the output of a given receptor or receptor type perfectly confounds changes in wavelength with changes in intensity because it has only one way of responding—that is, more or less. This is Rushton's Principle of Univariance—there is only one way of varying or one degree of freedom.

On the other hand, if we consider a visual system with two different receptor types, one more sensitive to longer wavelengths (L) and the other more sensitive to shorter wavelengths (S), there are two degrees of freedom in the system and thus the possibility of signalling our two independent variables—wavelength and intensity (Figure 16(b)). For example, if we summed the signals from the two different receptor types, L + S, the strength of the combined output would tell us something about the total amount of light reaching the two receptor types. If we subtracted the signals of one receptor type from the other, L – S, then more activation of L compared with S (L > S) would indicate that the spectral distribution of the light was skewed towards longer ('red') wavelengths and less activation of L compared with S, L < S, would indicate that the spectral distribution of the light was skewed towards shorter ('blue') wavelengths. Hence, it is quite possible to have a colour visual system that is based on just two receptor types. Such a colour visual system is referred to as dichromatic.

(a)

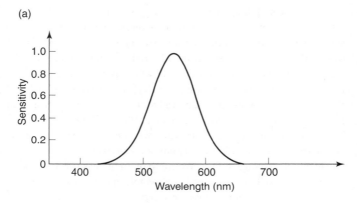

(b)

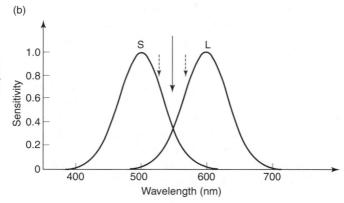

16. (a) A hypothetical spectral sensitivity curve of a single receptor type. (b) Hypothetical spectral sensitivity curves for two different receptor types (S and L). Light of a single wavelength (550 nm) (solid arrow) would produce a similar response in the two receptor types as would a combination of light of two different wavelengths (dashed arrows).

Metamerism

So why is the human visual system trichromatic? The answer can be found in a phenomenon known as *metamerism*. So far, we have restricted our discussion to the effect of a single wavelength on our dichromatic visual system: for example, a single wavelength of around 550 nm that stimulated both the long and short receptor types about equally: $(L - S) = 0$ (Figure 16(b)). But what would happen if we stimulated our dichromatic system with light of two different wavelengths at the same time—one long wavelength and one short wavelength? With a suitable choice of wavelengths, this combination of wavelengths would also have the effect of stimulating the two receptor types about equally: $(L - S) = 0$. As a consequence, the output of the system $(L - S)$ with this particular mixture of wavelengths would be indistinguishable from that created by the single wavelength of 550 nm. These two indistinguishable stimulus situations are referred to as metamers and a little thought shows that there would be many thousands of combinations of wavelengths that produce the same activity $(L - S)$ in a dichromatic visual system. As a consequence, all these different combinations of wavelengths would be indistinguishable to a dichromatic observer, even though they were produced by very different combinations of wavelengths. Moreover, because there are two degrees of freedom in a dichromatic visual system, it follows that a dichromat should be able to match any particular output of the system by varying the relative proportions of just two 'primaries' in a colour matching experiment and this turns out to be true in practice.

Is there any way of avoiding the problem of metamerism? The answer is no but we can make things better. If a visual system had three receptor types rather than two, then many of the combinations of wavelengths that produce an identical pattern of activity in two of the mechanisms (L and S) would create a different amount of activity in our third receptor type (M) that is maximally sensitive to medium wavelengths. Hence the number of indistinguishable metameric matches would be significantly reduced but they would never be eliminated. Using the same logic, it follows that a further increase in the number of receptor types (beyond three) would reduce the problem of metamerism even more and allow us to discriminate even more combinations of wavelengths or shades of colour. There would, however, also be a cost. Having more distinct receptor types in a finite-sized retina would increase the average spacing between the receptors of the same type and thus make our acuity for fine detail significantly poorer. There are many species, such as dragonflies, with more than three receptor types in their eyes but the larger number of receptor types typically serves to increase the range of wavelengths to which the animal is sensitive into the infra-red or ultra-violet parts of the spectrum, rather than to reduce the number of metamers.

As long as the spectral sensitivity functions of the three different receptor types overlap, we have three degrees of freedom or three independent dimensions in a trichromatic visual system. It follows that in a trichromatic visual system such as ours, it should be possible to match any given shade or combination of wavelengths with light consisting of just three different wavelengths (or combinations of wavelengths) and thus we have the answer to why Young's colour matching experiment provides evidence that the human visual system is trichromatic. However, close inspection of Figure 12 reveals that the sensitivity of the short wavelength receptors in the human eye only extends to ~540 nm—the S receptors are insensitive to longer wavelengths. This means that human colour vision is effectively dichromatic for combinations of wavelengths above 540 nm. In addition, there are no short wavelength cones in the central fovea of the human retina, which means that we are also dichromatic in the central part of our visual field. The fact that we are unaware of this lack of colour vision is probably due to the fact that our eyes are constantly moving.

Intensity, hue, and saturation

What implications does trichromacy have for the ability to describe and differentiate colours? The fact that we have three different (and independent) receptor types means that there is a triplet of numbers (corresponding to the outputs of the three receptor types) that specifies the 'colour' of a particular area of a scene. (Strictly speaking, we should say the light reflected from a particular visual direction, rather than the reflectance of a particular surface.) Note that this is the way that Photoshop and other image manipulation programs specify the colour of a local area—for instance 199 (red), 154 (green), 213 (blue) is used to create a particular shade of purple. But this is not a particularly useful or meaningful way to refer to the colour of a surface. I do not see the colour purple as a particular mixture of red, green, and blue light. Hence, it would be more useful to transform that triplet of numbers into something that makes more ecological sense. For example, it would be useful to separate out the overall amount of light reaching that part of the retina from its spectral characteristics. This could be done by summing the outputs of the three receptor types $(L + M + S)$ and taking two 'difference' or opponent signals $(L - M)$ and $((M + L) - S)$. This particular transformation of the receptor output signals is useful because it would allow the visual system to judge the 'colour' of a local area independently of the overall intensity of the light reaching the eye. The 19th-century physiologist Ewald Hering proposed that human colour vision is based on three 'opponent mechanisms'—red versus green: $L - M$; yellow versus blue: $(M + L) - S$; and white versus black: $L + M + S$, and there is good physiological evidence that a similar transformation is implemented in the visual systems of primates and humans. Note that this transformation retains the property of being a trichromatic system—there is still a triplet of numbers to code any particular input so that, in principle, no information is gained and no information is lost.

While it makes sense to separate out the intensity component from the two chromatic components, we do not typically think about the colours we perceive in terms of the relative amounts of red versus green $(L - M)$, and the relative amounts of yellow versus blue $((M + L) - S)$. Instead we tend to think of colours in terms of their hue and their saturation and this is the alternative way of specifying colours in Photoshop—hue, saturation, and brightness. For example, we regard red and a desaturated pink colour as having the same hue but with a different degree of saturation—the amount of whiteness in the colour. This could be done by a further transformation of the two difference signals into signals that correspond to hue and saturation.

Hence, by transforming the receptor signals in this way we arrive at a more useful description, in an ecological sense, of the properties of the light reaching a particular region of the retina—its *intensity*, *hue*, and *saturation*. Note that the description is still trichromatic—nothing is gained and nothing is lost from such a transformation. It is also important to appreciate that the description of the human colour visual system as trichromatic is not a description of the number of different receptor types in the retina—it is a property of the whole visual system. Psychophysical and behavioural techniques can only tell us about the properties of the whole system.

Individual differences

Recent research has shown that although the majority of humans are trichromatic there can be significant differences in the precise matches that individuals make when matching colour patches in the way described previously (Figure 15). The accepted explanation is that the peaks and/or the shapes of the three cone sensitive functions of these individuals may differ, particularly in the positions of the long and medium wave sensitivity functions (see Figure 12). If the peaks of an individual's long and medium wavelength sensitive cones are closer together than normal, this will result in poorer discrimination for wavelengths in the region between the two peaks. Such an individual would be described as colour anomalous. However, this small difference is unlikely to be noticed in everyday life. On the other hand, the absence of one receptor type will result in a greater number of colour confusions than normal and this does have a significant effect on an observer's colour vision. *Protanopia* is the absence of long wavelength receptors, *deuteranopia* the absence of medium wavelength receptors, and *tritanopia* the absence of short wavelength receptors. These three conditions are often described as 'colour blindness' but this is a misnomer. We are all colour blind to some extent because we all suffer from colour metamerism and fail to make discriminations that would be very apparent to any biological or machine vision system with a greater number of receptor types. For example, most stomatopod crustaceans (mantis shrimps) have twelve different visual pigments and they also have the ability to detect both linear and circularly polarized light. What I find interesting is that we believe, as trichromats, that we have the ability to discriminate all the possible shades of colour (reflectance characteristics) that exist in our world. But note that this kind of chauvinism is a characteristic of all our perceptual abilities—we are typically unaware of the limitations of our visual systems because we have no way of comparing what we see normally with what would be seen by a 'better' visual system. I never noticed my increasing short-sightedness until I tried on a pair of glasses to correct it!

Chapter 4
Motion perception

The ability to detect motion is one of the most important properties of our visual system and the visual systems of nearly every other species. Motion perception is not just important for detecting the movement of objects in the surrounding world—both for catching prey and for avoiding predators—but it is also important for providing information about the 3-D structure of the surrounding world; for maintaining balance; determining our direction of heading; segregating the scene and breaking camouflage; and judging time-to-contact with other objects in the world. Gibson proposed the useful distinction between *exterospecific* information—information about the properties of the surrounding world—and *propriospecific* information—information about our own movements within that world.

Motion as a spatio-temporal process

Motion detection is necessarily a spatio-temporal process. Motion cannot be detected by monitoring the light from a single direction in space or from the spatial pattern of light at a single moment in time. These constraints suggest that the simplest model of motion detection would involve detecting the light coming from two different directions in space at two or more instants in time. For the compound eyes of most insects, this would entail detecting the time-varying activity of two ommatidia directed towards two different regions of space. For the chambered eye of birds and mammals (including humans), this would entail detecting the time-varying activity of two spatially separated receptors in the retina.

Consider the detection of motion with a stationary eye. The motion of a light–dark contour, such as the boundary of a light object seen against a darker background, will initially cause an increase in the amount of light falling on one receptor followed (slightly later) by an increase of light falling on a second (spatially separated) receptor. Therefore, the task of the visual system is to detect the *temporal correlation* (correlation over time) of the increased (or decreased) activity in the two receptors. One possible implementation of such a model would be to introduce a slight delay to the output of the first receptor so that the delayed output of the first receptor would reach a correlation detector at the same time as the undelayed output of the second receptor (Figure 17). If the two inputs to the detector are summed or multiplied together, the detector's response would be maximal when the delayed output from the first detector arrives at the same time as the undelayed output of the second detector. Thus, our simple motion detector would not only respond selectively to motion in a particular direction but would also be tuned to a particular velocity that depends on the spatial separation of the detectors and the size of the temporal delay.

Based on the properties of the frog visual system, Horace Barlow and William Levick proposed a motion model that either added or subtracted the outputs of two receptors, one of which was delayed in time (Figure 17(a)). Werner Reichardt and Bernhard Hassenstein suggested an alternative model based on multiplication that was inspired by characteristics of the beetle visual system (Figure 17(b)). A complete system of motion detection would also require detectors sensitive to the opposite direction of motion, as well as

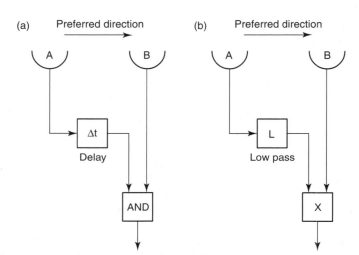

17. Models of motion detection: (a) Barlow and Levick's model based on summing the output of receptor B to the delayed output of receptor A. (b) Reichardt and Hassenstein's model based on multiplying the output of receptor B to the low pass filtered (delayed) output of receptor A.

receptors separated in different directions, in order to detect motion in any direction. These models of motion detection are referred to as *sequence models*. An inevitable consequence of monitoring the activity of two spatially separated receptors is that the model would also respond to an increase in the amount of light falling on the first detector followed by an increase in the amount of light falling on the second receptor, in the absence of any actual motion in the world. The probability of this occurring in the real world is minimal but the consequence is inevitable. It would be possible to minimize the chance of this happening by having the two receptors that provide the inputs to the motion detector as close together as possible. On the other hand, it would be advantageous to have the receptors further apart so that the motion of objects and boundaries moving at high velocities could be extracted more reliably because the delay between stimulation of the two receptors would be longer.

Apparent motion

The discussion in the section 'Motion as a spatio-temporal process' suggests that any implementation of a sequence model of motion detection would necessarily signal motion inappropriately when the amount of light reaching a single receptor in the retina of a chambered eye (or one ommatidium in a compound eye) was increased and was followed by an increase in the amount of light reaching a second, spatially separated receptor in the retina (or a different ommatidium in a compound eye). However, this is precisely what happens in human vision. In the last decade of the 19th century, Sigmund Exner reported that human observers saw motion when a spot of light in a particular visual direction was turned on and then off followed by the turning on and off of a second light in a slightly different visual direction. This perceptual effect is referred to as the phi phenomenon or more generally as apparent motion. Several years later, Adolph Korte established the spatial and temporal parameters over which apparent motion can be seen. Although the susceptibility of the human visual system to apparent motion might be seen as an unfortunate perceptual consequence, it has been exploited very successfully in movies and television. In both cases, a series of separate (non-moving) images (frames) is presented in quick succession and as long as the displacement of the contours in successive frames is not too great and the interval between the successive presentations is not too long, we are 'fooled' into seeing continuous motion.

The motion after-effect

Apparent motion provides us with a good example of how a perceptual effect can tell us something about the characteristics of the underlying mechanisms. In the 1820s, the Czech scientist Jan Purkyně noted another important perceptual effect. He described seeing motion in the opposite direction—a motion after-effect—after watching a cavalry parade of soldiers marching in front of him.

A few years later, Robert Addams noticed that after watching the flow of water down the Falls of Foyers in Scotland, there was an after-effect of motion in an upward direction when he transferred his gaze to the stationary rocks alongside—an effect referred to as the waterfall illusion. What can account for these motion after-effects? The usual explanation is that retinal motions produced by the marching soldiers, or the flowing water, stimulate a subset of motion detectors that respond to the particular direction of motion. If we assume that these motion detectors adapt with continual exposure (so that their output signals are attenuated) and that the detectors have some background rate of responding in the absence of motion then, when the motion is stopped, the background activity of the motion detectors signalling motion in the opposite direction will be higher than the attenuated activity of the motion detectors signalling motion in the same direction as the original stimulation. This explanation is supported by the findings of Horace Barlow and Richard Hill, who found that cells in the rabbit retina showed a decrease in the rate of responding after being stimulated with continuous motion for thirty seconds.

Why should motion detectors show adaptation with continual stimulation? A possible explanation is fatigue—the motion detectors are simply unable to respond because they are 'worn out' in the same way that our muscles become fatigued after strenuous activity. A more plausible story, however, is that the adaptation is part of an active process of recalibration, not dissimilar to the light and dark adaptation of receptors in the retina with changing light levels. All sensory and motor systems need to be able to adjust to the changing conditions of the external world and match their sensitivities and responses to the current situation. In the case of motion perception, the input to the motion system will normally average to 'stationary' over time—that is, no net motion in any particular direction—but if the input is biased over a period of time away from that norm, the system adapts by changing the norm with the consequence that we see motion in the opposite direction for a few seconds afterwards until the 'stationary' norm is restored.

Induced motion

There is a third perceptual effect—induced motion—that tells us something about the characteristics of the motion system. If you look at the moon on a cloudy night when the clouds are moving rapidly across the moon's surface, the moon appears to move in the opposite direction. This effect is referred to as *induced motion* because the apparent motion of the moon is induced by the motion of the surrounding clouds. But what would be the benefit to an animal of a coding strategy that produces this inappropriate perceptual effect? Like most animals, we are foveating creatures—meaning that we look at things of interest and typically follow or track objects with movements of our head and eyes. As a consequence, the absence of motion of an image across our retinas is not a reliable signal of whether the object has or has not moved in the world. On the other hand, the relative motion between a tracked object and its background provides a reliable signal of their relative motion. Given that the world surrounding us is generally stationary (including the ground plane on which we stand), it makes sense to 'attribute' the relative motion to the object rather than the surroundings. In the last century, Karl Duncker showed that the motion of a simple outline frame that surrounds a stationary point is sufficient to produce the appearance of motion of the point in the opposite direction to the motion of the frame. The larger the area of the surrounding motion, the more powerful the perception of the induced motion (Figure 18).

So far, we have only considered how we use retinal motion to tell us about object movement but, as pointed out at the beginning of this chapter, there are many other uses of retinal motion.

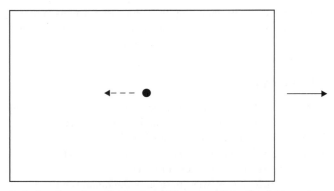

18. Induced motion—the motion of the rectangle to the right creates the impression that the spot in the centre is moving to the left.

Motion for segregating the world

We take it for granted that we are able to segregate the visual input into separate objects and distinguish objects from their backgrounds and we rarely make mistakes except under impoverished conditions. How is this possible? In many cases, the boundaries of objects are defined by changes of luminance and colour and these changes allow us to separate or segregate an object from its background. But luminance and colour changes are also present in the textured surfaces of many objects and therefore we need to ask how it is that our visual system does not mistake these luminance and colour changes for the boundaries of objects. One answer is that object boundaries have special characteristics. In our world, most objects and surfaces are opaque and hence they occlude (cover) the surface of the background. As a consequence, the contours of the background surface typically end—they are 'terminated'—at the boundary of the occluding object or surface. Quite often, the occluded contours of the background are also revealed at the opposite side of the occluding surface because they are physically continuous. Barbara Gillam's elegant demonstrations have shown that both these factors

(a)   (b)

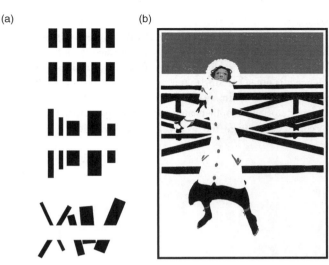

19. (a) Barbara Gillam's occluding and occluded contours. In the top row, there is only a weak impression of the edges of a (white) surface obscuring the black bars. In the middle row, the impression of the edges of an occluding surface is stronger when the bars have different lengths and widths and all the bars are stopped (terminated) along the same horizontal contours. The strongest impression is produced when the bars have different orientations as well as different lengths and widths, as in the bottom row. (b) A Collier's magazine cover from 1910 showing how the terminations of the black background lines are sufficient to define the outline contour of the occluding figure. (My thanks to Peter Tse for alerting me to this image.)

influence the probability of seeing a surface as separate and occluding (Figure 19(a)). Moreover, the impression of occlusion is enhanced if the occluded contours contain a range of different lengths, widths, and orientations. In the natural world, many animals use colour and texture to camouflage their boundaries as well as to fool potential predators about their identity.

There is an additional source of information—relative motion—that can be used to segregate a visual scene into objects and their backgrounds and to break any camouflage that might exist in a static view. A moving, opaque object will progressively occlude and dis-occlude (reveal) the background surface so that even a well-camouflaged, moving animal will give away its location. Hence it is not surprising that a very common and successful strategy of many animals is to freeze in order not to be seen. Unless the predator has a sophisticated visual system to break the pattern or colour camouflage, the prey will remain invisible.

Chapter 5
Perception of a 3-D world

The traditional perspective

The ability to perceive the 3-D world has often been regarded as a task that poses particular problems for the visual system. This view can be traced back to the philosopher George Berkeley who wrote in his book *Towards a New Theory of Vision* that:

> *distance* of itself, and immediately, cannot be seen.

Some authors have claimed that the problem of 3-D vision arises because the retinal image is only a two-dimensional surface and therefore information about the depth and distance of objects and surfaces is somehow missing. For example, Irvin Rock has written:

> If we possessed a three-dimensional retina and a mechanism that registered the distance of a thing by its location in such a retina, our ability to perceive depth might be less remarkable. But the human retina is effectively a two-dimensional surface.

This idea is misleading and the error is in assuming that the dimensionality of the retina—a two-dimensional surface—is the factor that limits our ability to perceive the 3-D world. The more appropriate starting point for understanding 3-D vision is to consider the information that is available in the optic array that subsequently creates our retinal images. The light reflected from objects and surfaces in the surrounding world reaches a particular vantage point (or viewing position) from many different directions and any visual system that has to extract information about the spatial changes of light in the world—the contours, boundaries, and textures of objects—requires mechanisms to detect those changes. Those contours may be present in a retinal image but they need to be extracted or made 'explicit', to use Marr's terminology. In the case of a simple, chambered eye, like the mammalian eye, this can be achieved by comparing the outputs of neighbouring receptors. For compound eyes, like those of insects, this can be achieved by comparing the outputs of neighbouring ommatidia.

But note that information about the spatial changes of light in the world can be extracted even when there is no extended array of receptors or ommatidia. The copepod *Copilia quadrata*, studied by Sigmund Exner in the 19th century, has a pair of eyes (each containing a small number of receptors) that are capable of making small side-to-side scanning movements. This allows the receptors to scan the pattern of light reaching the eye from different directions. In the case of *Copilia*, information about spatial changes of light in the surrounding world is captured in the temporal pattern of activity. Note that this is how the image of the world is captured on a traditional TV camera. In other words, a spatial image is not necessary for capturing spatial information. The key to understanding a perceptual system lies in first identifying the information that is available in the optic array before considering the properties of a particular perceptual system and whether it is capable of extracting that information.

3-D information

In the case of human 3-D vision, the correct question to ask is: 'what information is available in the optic array(s) reaching our eyes that can tell us about the 3-D structure of the surrounding world?' If we lived in a world of isolated points or stars, the answer is provided by geometry: there is no information about the distance of individual points reaching a single vantage point. The fact that the retinal image is 2-D is irrelevant—having a 'three-dimensional retina' would not help. This is evident in our perception of the stars in the night sky—they all appear to be at the same distance from us and there is no way that we (or any other seeing machine) could perceive their actual distances from a single vantage point. Note that this was the situation to which Berkeley was referring—a world of isolated points—and has nothing to do with the retinal image being 2-D. He made this clear when he went on to add:

> For *distance* being a line directed end-wise to the eye, it projects only one point in the fund [back] of the eye. Which point remains invariably the same, whether the distance be longer or shorter.

Perspective

Fortunately, we do not live in a world of isolated points. We live in a world of surfaces and the patterns of light from those surfaces reaching a single vantage point provide 3-D information. One of the major sources of information is *perspective* which is a consequence of the geometry of projection. The angular extent of an object varies inversely with its distance from a vantage point—to a first approximation the angular extent of that object halves if we double the distance to the object—this is Euclid's law (Figure 20). One of the consequences of the perspective projection at a vantage point is that the angular separation between two straight and parallel lines in the world varies over the lengths of the lines as a result of the different distances to the lines—this is referred to as linear perspective.

A second consequence of perspective is that a textured surface in the surrounding world creates a gradient of angular size in the

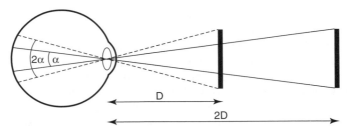

20. Doubling the distance of an object from the eye halves its angular size and thus the size of the image on the retina.

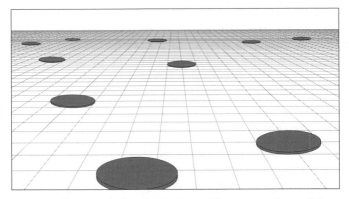

21. A receding, textured surface in the world creates gradients of size, density (number of elements in a given region), and foreshortening (the width-to-height ratio of the elements) in the optic array (and retinal image). In addition, the covering or occlusion of the surface by opaque objects provides information about their depth order.

optic array. These optic array properties can, of course, be expressed in terms of their retinal image properties—parallel lines in the world converge in the retinal image, and a textured surface in the world creates a texture gradient across the retinal image (Figure 21). However, it is important to remember that these geometric properties exist in the optic array quite independently of the properties of any particular visual system.

Occlusion

A second source of information about the spatial layout of surfaces in the world comes from the fact that most natural surfaces in the world are opaque—they do not let light through. As a consequence, objects and surfaces that are closer to the vantage point obscure the light from more distant objects. Note that occlusion information in the optic array does not provide any information about the quantitative difference in distance between the occluding and occluded surfaces, just their depth order. The information for occlusion comes from the way the background contours are terminated by the occluding surface (Figures 19 and 21).

Shape-from-shading

A third potential source of information about the 3-D structure of the world comes from the pattern of light that is reflected from a 3-D surface. If the reflectance characteristic of a particular surface is even (i.e. homogeneous)—like the skin covering our faces—simple physics tells us that the amount of light reflected from a homogeneous (*Lambertian*) surface varies with the cosine of the angle of the surface to the incident illumination and is independent of the location of the observer. More light is reflected from the parts of the surface that are orthogonal to the direction of illumination and less light from parts of the surface that are slanted with respect to the direction of illumination. This is the basis of shape-from-shading information.

The word shape is important because shape-from-shading information cannot tell us about absolute distance (like the convergence angle of the eyes), or depth (like binocular disparities—see the section 'Binocular stereopsis') or even depth gradients (like perspective). Instead, shape-from-shading provides information about the changes of depth gradients of surfaces—their shapes or curvatures—as is evident in the

22. The principal source of information about the shape of Voltaire's head comes from the shading pattern.

sculpture of Voltaire (Figure 22). Note that skin has very little texture (at a visible scale) that would otherwise create perspective gradients and there are very few sharp contours (edges) to provide us with binocular disparity information. As a consequence, shape-from-shading information is probably the most important source of information for judging the 3-D structure of faces and sculptures. However, if the lighting is diffuse and comes from multiple directions, as is often true of theatre stage lighting, 3-D structures such as faces no longer create shading patterns. As a consequence, actors have to rely on stage make-up to recreate the naturally occurring patterns of shading.

The traditional view of perception, with its assumption of the insufficiency of the available information, has led many writers to emphasize the ambiguity of shape-from-shading information. For example, the shading pattern produced by a protruding, convex 3-D surface can be the same as, or very similar to, that produced by a hollow, concave surface. So we might expect there to be ambiguity in what we perceive but this is not the case. The circular patches in the upper two rows of Figure 23 are seen (correctly) as a series of convex mounds and those in the lower two rows as a series of concave hollows. The reason why the ambiguity goes away is either that there is information about the direction of the lighting or that we 'assume' the direction of lighting is from above.

If this is the case, the shading pattern in the upper rows of Figure 23 could only be created by a series of convex mounds and the shading pattern in the lower rows could only be created by a series of concave hollows. Note that it is not necessary to think that there is anything high-level about the 'assumption' that the direction of lighting is from above. Indeed, we are typically unaware of the direction of the illumination, even when we are asked to judge it explicitly. However, our visual systems have evolved in a world where the principal direction of the illumination is from above and, as a consequence, it is better thought of as a constraint rather than a (cognitive) assumption.

The 'lighting from above' constraint does not always constrain what we see and faces appear to be an exception. The photo on the left in Figure 24 is of a normal convex face whereas the photo on the right is of a hollow (concave) mask. However, both appear as

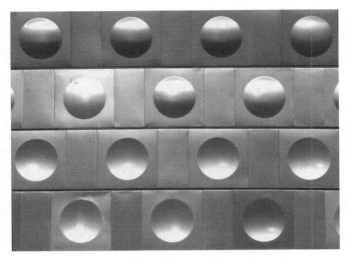

23. The bumps and hollows on the wall of a Prague Metro station. The shading patterns in the upper two rows are seen (correctly) as convex bumps and the shading patterns in the lower two rows as concave hollows (correctly). If you turn the book upside down, the previously seen hollows will now look like bumps and vice versa for the previously seen bumps.

normal convex faces. Why should this be? This effect has been explained as a consequence of our lifetime's exposure to normal, protruding faces and the complete absence of hollow faces in the world. In support of this explanation, it has been found that upside-down hollow faces are more likely to be seen as hollow than upright hollow faces. Alternatively, it has been suggested that the effect is a consequence of the statistical fact that there are more protruding than hollow structures in the world and that our visual systems have evolved over generations to exploit this particular statistical property of the world. Support for this alternative explanation comes from the finding that hollow versions of many three-dimensional surfaces (and not just faces) are typically seen as protruding.

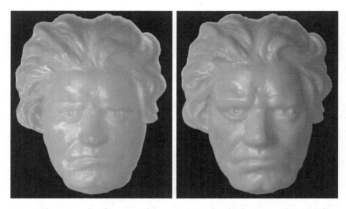

24. A photograph of a normal (convex) mask of a face (Beethoven), lit from the left-hand side, and a photograph of the back view of the same mask, lit from the right-hand side, which appears convex but is actually hollow (concave).

Cues and clues

In many textbooks on perception, these three (monocular) sources of information—perspective, occlusion, and shading—are referred to as *painters' cues* because they can be exploited by artists wishing to create an impression of depth in flat paintings and drawings. However, the idea of painters' cues can be misleading. The basis of these cues lies in the physics and geometry of the world we live in and the information they provide is not limited to paintings and drawings. The word 'cue'—meaning a hint or a prompt—is also misleading because it suggests that there is some uncertainty or ambiguity about the information these cues provide. This uncertainty and ambiguity is often demonstrated with examples such as the Ames Room (Figure 1), the hollow face (Figure 24), and Itelson's playing card experiment (Figure 25). All three are examples of *equivalent configurations*—situations in which the same retinal image can be created by a variety of different 3-D scenarios. A little thought, however, shows that these equivalent configurations actually demonstrate the power of those

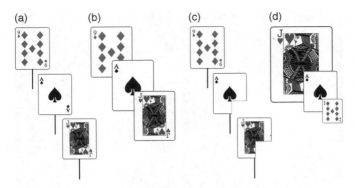

25. Itelson's playing card experiment. (a) When the playing cards are lined up so that the nearer cards cover (occlude) the more distant cards, we see their depth order correctly (b). However, when the cards are positioned so that the cut-outs of the nearer cards line up with the edges of the more distant cards (c), we see the depth order as indicated by the occlusion information even though this contradicts their (assumed) identical sizes (d).

sources of information—the power of perspective in the case of the Ames Room, the power of shading in the case of the hollow face, and the power of occlusion in the case of Itelson's playing card experiment—rather than demonstrating the uncertainty or ambiguity of the so-called depth cues. This issue is discussed in more detail in Chapter 7 on illusions.

It is important to remember that we have evolved in a world of textured and opaque surfaces and these surfaces are typically viewed under particular illumination conditions. Therefore, it should not surprise us to learn that our perceptual systems have evolved to take advantage of these particular constraints and characteristics of the world in order to survive. The fact that we very rarely experience difficulties in judging the 3-D structure of objects in the world and their layout provides strong evidence that the patterns of light reaching our eyes provide rich information to a visual system that has successfully evolved to exploit and extract that information.

Information from more than one vantage point

So far, we have only considered the information about the structure and layout of the 3-D world that is available at a *single vantage point* and ignored the 3-D information that is available from two or more vantage points. If we think about our own visual systems, we have two spatially separated eyes that are capable of picking up the binocular information that is present in the two (different) optic arrays from two spatially separated vantage points. However, before we discuss the information that binocular stereopsis provides, it is important to point out that the overwhelming majority of animals do not have forward-facing eyes, like ours, with overlapping visual fields and, as a consequence, they are not able to exploit the binocular information available to animals with forward-facing eyes.

Motion parallax

Although animals with laterally placed eyes are not able to exploit the information present in the optic arrays at two spatially separated viewing positions, those animals can move and change their viewing position and those movements necessarily create changes in a single optic array. In the simplest case, the side-to-side movements of an observer will create relative motion in the optic array (and subsequently in the retinal image) between objects at different distances—this relative motion is referred to as *motion parallax*. For many centuries, astronomers have made use of the same geometric property to judge the relative distances of the stars by exploiting the parallax displacements between stars created at different moments during the earth's orbit around the sun. The far smaller movements of an animal also create relative motion between objects located at different distances from the animal and this relative motion provides information about their 3-D locations in space.

(a)

(b)

26. (a) When an observer is fixating a point in the far distance and walking from the right to the left, there is an inverse relationship between the distance and the amount of parallax motion (shown by the arrows). (b) When the observer is fixating a nearer point, the parallax motion is in the *opposite* direction to the observer's movement for points closer to the observer than the fixation point and in the *same* direction for points further away than the fixation point.

In optic array terms, an object at infinity creates no motion in the optic array when the vantage point moves because the angular direction of a distant object does not change. For objects that are closer than infinity, there is an inverse relationship between the angular speed of motion and the distance of the object (Figure 26(a)). However, because our eyes can move and we typically fixate or track a particular object, the parallax motions on the retinal image are quite different: the image of the fixated object will always remain stationary on the retina; the images of objects closer to the observer displace in the opposite direction to the observer's movement; and the images of objects further away displace in the same direction (Figure 26(b)).

The motion parallax created when an animal or observer moves can be referred to as observer-produced parallax. The movement of a 3-D object across our line of sight also creates relative motion in the optic array (and the retinal image) between the parts of the object that are at different distances from the observer. This is referred to as object-produced motion parallax. It is also important to remember that we live in a world of surfaces, rather than isolated points, and as a consequence 3-D surfaces don't just create relative motion between points, they create continuous gradients of motion in the optic array both when the observer moves (Figure 26) and when 3-D objects move with respect to the observer. My own experiments with Maureen Graham showed that those gradients of motion—which Gibson referred to as *motion perspective*—are sufficient to produce a powerful and unambiguous impression of the 3-D structure of a surface under both observer- and object-produced viewing conditions. There is also good evidence that other species are able to utilize motion parallax information. Eric Sobell has shown that locusts use side-to-side swaying movements before jumping from one surface to another and Mel Goodale and his colleagues have shown that gerbils use head-bobbing before jumping to an unfamiliar target. In both cases, the movements of the animal create parallax motions that provide information about the 3-D layout of the surrounding scene.

Optic flow

It is important to remember that we are terrestrial creatures and we move around on a ground plane surface. As a consequence, it seems very likely that the motion perspective created by the ground plane surface when we move plays an important role in detecting its 3-D properties—for example allowing us to walk or run over a sloping or an undulating surface without stumbling. As yet, there have been very few studies that have investigated this particular aspect of motion parallax. The changes in the optic array that are created by observer or object motion represent aspects of what is referred to as *optic flow*, and the elegant mathematical analyses of Jan Koenderink and Andrea van Doorn as well as Christopher Longuet-Higgins have confirmed that the transforming optic array provides information about the 3-D structure of objects and their layout. Optic flow also has the potential to provide us with information about our own movements in the visual world and examples of this can be seen in the way we maintain balance and in our perception of self-motion. These aspects will be discussed in detail in Chapter 6, but suffice to say that the experimental evidence supports the view that optic flow plays an important role in the maintenance of balance, the perception of self-motion, and the perceived direction of heading.

Binocular stereopsis

The optic flow created by a moving animal contains information about the 3-D structure and layout of the surrounding world for most animals but for species with two forward-facing eyes, with overlap in their visual fields, there is an additional source of information—binocular stereopsis. Like motion parallax, the information exists by virtue of the underlying geometry: the optic arrays created by the surrounding 3-D world and reaching two spatially separated vantage points are necessarily different. As a consequence, the images projected onto the retinas of human observers are different and these differences are referred to as *binocular disparities*.

What information do these disparities provide? Binocular disparities and motion parallax share much in common: for an object located at infinity, the visual direction is identical in the optic arrays from two spatially separated viewing positions just as there is no change in visual direction when a single viewing position moves from side to side. Like motion parallax, there is an inverse relationship between the distance of a closer object and the size of its angular disparity. As a consequence, the differences between the optic arrays have the potential to provide information about absolute distance, but are we able to use it? There is evidence that animals such as owls are able to use retinal disparities to judge absolute distance but owls are unusual in that their eyes do not move with respect to their heads. The situation is quite different for the visual systems of other animals, including humans, where the eyes can converge and diverge in order to fixate (look at) objects at different distances. As a consequence, the retinal disparity of the fixated object will always be close to zero, whether the object is closer or further away, and thus the horizontal disparity of the fixated object, by itself, cannot tell us about absolute distance. However, objects that are either closer to the observer than the fixation point or further away do create retinal disparities and these disparities provide us with relative distance or depth information. For objects that are closer than the fixation point, these differences are referred to as convergent (or crossed) disparities and for objects that are more distant than the fixation point, divergent (or uncrossed) disparities. The amount of disparity can be expressed as the difference between the vergence angle of the fixation point (α) and the vergence angle that would be required to fixate a disparate point in the scene (β) (Figure 27).

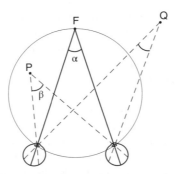

27. The loci of all points that have zero disparity lie on a circle through the fixation point and the optic centres of the two eyes—the Vieth-Müller circle. Any point within the V-M circle creates a convergent binocular disparity and any point outside the V-M circle creates a divergent disparity. The angular disparity of point P is: α–β.

Strictly speaking, retinal disparities only tell us about the locations of objects with respect to a circle passing through the optical centres of the two eyes and the fixated object, which is known as the Vieth-Müller circle. But there is another complication. The retinal disparities created by a particular object vary with the viewing distance and therefore they do not provide any information, by themselves, about the amount of depth in the object. To a first approximation, disparities vary inversely with the square of the absolute distance—a relationship known as the *inverse square law*. If the absolute distance to an object is doubled, the disparities created by that 3-D object will be reduced to one-quarter of their original value. This means that binocular disparities are particularly useful for making depth judgements at close distances and much less useful at far distances where the disparities become vanishing small. (Note that this effect is similar to the inverse relationship between the physical size of a particular object and its angular size, described in the section 'Perspective'.) Traditionally, it has been assumed that in order to recover information about both the size and the depth of an object, the angular sizes and angular retinal disparities have to be 'scaled' by some estimate of the absolute distance to an object in order to 'achieve' size and depth constancy.

Eye vergence and depth constancy

Information about absolute distance could be derived from the vergence state of the eyes—acting like a range finder—and, in principle, this could be used for both size and depth scaling (Figure 28(a)). Experiments have shown that the apparent size of an object changes when the vergence state of the eyes is manipulated—the apparent size decreases as the vergence angle increases—an effect known as *micropsia*. Do changes of vergence angle have a similar effect on the perceived depth from binocular disparities? When only a single cylindrical surface is visible in an otherwise dark room and the vergence angle between the eyes is the only source of absolute distance information, Elizabeth Johnston found that there was some compensation for the changing distance but the extent of constancy was very poor, corresponding to only 25 per cent of that required for a complete compensation.

These results tell us about our ability to judge the size and depth of a single object or surface but we might question whether size and depth scaling is always necessary for perceiving the world around us. It could be argued that the more important information is the relative size and the relative depth of two or more similar objects at different distances. In principle, this is a much easier task because geometry shows that we only need information about the relative distances to the different objects, rather than their absolute distances. Andrew Glennerster, Mark Bradshaw, and I have shown that depth constancy is much better when making these comparative judgements.

Vertical disparities and differential perspective

So far, I have considered the geometry of the *horizontal* disparities that are the consequence of having two spatially separated eyes or

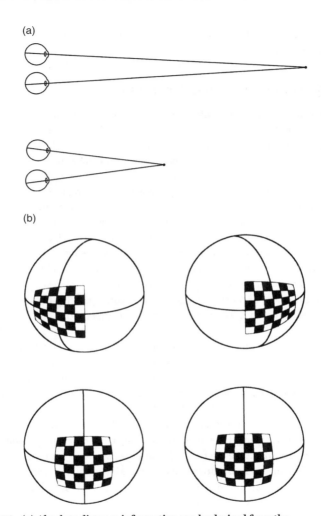

28. (a) Absolute distance information can be derived from the
vergence angle of the two eyes needed to fixate an object that is either
further away or closer to the observer. (b) Absolute distance
information can also be derived from the perspective views of a
chessboard pattern viewed from two spatially separated vantage
points. For a surface close to the observer, the two perspective views
are quite different (upper images) whereas for a surface at infinity,
the two perspective views are the same (lower images).

vantage points. Indeed, most of the differences between the two retinal images are in a horizontal direction because the eyes are separated horizontally. However, geometry shows that there are also differences in the vertical locations of points in the optic arrays from two spatially separated vantage points. These differences are referred to as *vertical disparities*. Consider viewing a square chessboard pattern from a close distance (Figure 28(b)). The left-hand edge of the chessboard pattern is larger in angular size for the left vantage point (or left eye) than for the right because it is closer and, conversely, the right-hand edge of the pattern is smaller for the left vantage point (or left eye) than for the right because it is further away.

Figure 28(b) shows that the two eyes receive slightly different perspective views of the chessboard and the absolute distance information they provide can be referred to as *differential perspective*. For any continuous surface like the chessboard, there is a horizontal gradient of the ratio of the vertical sizes in the two eyes and this varies with viewing distance. From a very large distance, the angular sizes of the left- and right-hand edges of the pattern are the same and, as a consequence, there is no horizontal gradient of the ratio of the vertical sizes in the two eyes. It follows that the gradient of this ratio—the amount of differential perspective—provides information about the absolute distance to the chessboard or any other surface, as was first suggested by Barbara Gillam and Bo Lawergren.

Analysis of the underlying geometry of binocular vision shows that the gradient of relative vertical sizes—the differential perspective—provides information about the absolute distance to a surface but it is an empirical question as to whether this information is used by humans or any other species. My own research with Mark Bradshaw provided the first evidence that we are able to exploit vertical disparity information by artificially manipulating the amount of differential perspective. Using a task in which observers had to judge the amount of depth in a wavy surface, we found that observers perceived more depth when the differential perspective indicated a larger distance and less depth when the gradient indicated a closer distance. Our overall conclusion was that both the vergence angle of the eyes and differential perspective contribute to the perception of depth in 3-D objects and surfaces.

Primary and secondary depth cues

There are many different sources of information about the 3-D structure of objects and their layout that contribute to our perception of a 3-D world but are they equally effective? The conventional wisdom is that the monocular sources of information, referred to as 'painters' cues', are secondary and less important than the primary cues of eye vergence, accommodation (focusing the image), binocular disparity, and motion parallax. Moreover, it is often assumed that the secondary cues like perspective and shape-from-shading have to be learned as a result of our experience of the world. But why should we have to learn to use those secondary sources of information? It is very likely that our ability to use any source of 3-D information will be refined or 'tuned-up' as a result of experience (like other aspects of our perception), but because the geometric consequences of perspective, occlusion, and shape-from-shading have always been present in the world, it seems unlikely that we would have to wait until we are born to learn how to use that information. In principle, the role of learning could be answered by testing the visual abilities of young babies but, in practice, there are difficulties in carrying out such studies and the maturational factors in perceptual development complicate the situation. We have to learn how to use perspective and shading when attempting to paint a picture but this is quite different from the assumption that the visual system needs to learn how to use these characteristics of the world in order to perceive the 3-D properties of the world.

Two of the traditional primary cues—convergence and accommodation—are different from the remaining cues in that their 3-D information is derived from proprioceptive or motor signals, rather than from image characteristics. However, the experimental evidence shows that, rather than being primary, both these cues are rather poor for making absolute distance judgements. We might also question why binocular stereopsis and motion parallax are regarded as primary cues. The information they provide is based on image characteristics—the differences between the two retinal images for binocular stereopsis and the changes in the retinal image over time for motion parallax. It seems to me that the traditional distinction between primary and secondary cues confuses two different issues—(i) the nature and reliability of the available information (the computational theory) and (ii) our ability to use the information. In principle, the convergence angle between the eyes (Figure 28(a)) could be a very accurate and precise source of absolute distance information (and has been exploited in camera focusing mechanisms) but, in practice, the mechanisms in the human visual system for extracting the convergence angle do not provide reliable and accurate distance information for human observers. On the other hand, the perspective information that is regarded as a mere painters' cue turns out to be a very reliable and powerful source of 3-D information.

The effectiveness of different sources of 3-D information

What do we know about the effectiveness of these different sources of information? It is often assumed that binocular disparities provide the most important and precise information about the 3-D structure and layout of objects in the world. Moreover, the invention of the stereoscope by Charles Wheatstone in the 1830s provided good evidence that binocular disparities produce a vivid impression of depth and distance (Figure 41). More recently, the

TV manufacturers have tried to persuade us to buy '3-D TVs' so that we can enjoy a 'true 3-D experience'. The mistaken assumption is that the pictures on an ordinary TV do not provide sufficient 3-D information for our perceptual systems. This is not true. Try watching TV (or films in cinemas) with just one eye and you will see considerable depth in the depicted scene, particularly when the camera taking the images is moving. The problem is that a conventional TV picture also provides contradictory evidence—binocular disparities—and this tells us that the picture is flat. If the contradictory information is removed, the scene appears in depth.

Further evidence of the relative effectiveness of monocular and binocular sources of information in the human perceptual system has come from the Reverspective artworks of the British artist Patrick Hughes. Instead of painting on a flat canvas, Reverspectives are painted on a series of truncated pyramids and wedges that extend out of the picture plane towards the viewer (Figure 29). On the sides of the pyramids and wedges, Hughes has painted the perspective images of receding buildings and streets and these provide information that the 3-D structure recedes away from the viewer. On the other hand, the 'true' 3-D structure comes out towards the viewer—hence the name Reverspective. What does the viewer see? Unless the viewer is very close to a Reverspective, we see the 3-D structure given by the perspective information rather than the physical 3-D structure given by the binocular disparities and the vergence angle of the eyes. Moreover, the impression of depth in the direction specified by the perspective information is enhanced if the viewer moves from side to side or up and down. Why should this be? The answer is that the 3-D structure of a Reverspective also creates motion parallax between parts of the artwork that are closer to and further away from the viewer when the viewer moves from side to side. The only real-world scenario that would create the impression of a 3-D structure that recedes away from the observer, but with parallax motions that would normally be created

(a)

(b)

29. (a) A Patrick Hughes Reverspective. (b) An oblique view of the same Reverspective showing that it consists of truncated pyramids that project out from the background.

by the protruding 3-D structure, is a 3-D structure that rotates with (i.e. in the same direction as) the viewer's movements. And this is what we see.

To use a bad pun, Reverspectives put binocular disparities into perspective. Perspective information can, and often does, dominate over binocular disparities and Reverspectives provide important new evidence of the power and effectiveness of both perspective and motion parallax information for our perceptual systems. However, it is also true that binocular disparities are capable of providing very precise information about the 3-D structure of objects and surfaces at close distances and this information is particularly useful for certain practical tasks. This illustrates a very important point—different sources of 3-D information are useful in different circumstances and for performing different tasks.

Bringing together the different sources of 3-D information

So far, we have discussed the different sources of 3-D information that are present in the surrounding world and from this we might assume that there are separate mechanisms in the brain to extract the different sorts of information. If true, there must be mechanisms that combine the different sources of information in order to provide us with a single, unified percept of the 3-D world. To study the mechanisms involved in combining different sorts of 3-D information, researchers have created cue-combination paradigms in which two different sources of 3-D information are presented to the observer, each of which signals a slightly different 3-D property, such as the slant (or curvature) of a surface. The observer is required to match the perceived slant of the surface to some comparison surface. The results show that observers typically match the perceived slant to lie somewhere in between the values of the two discrepant cues. The bias towards the value indicated by one cue or the other is taken as evidence that the human visual system computes some sort of weighted average of the two cues. It is also assumed that the magnitude of the respective weights depends on the relative reliability of the two cues. For example, the slant indicated by binocular disparities might be more heavily weighted than texture gradient information when the surface slant is close to the frontal (vertical) plane whereas for slants closer to the horizontal plane, texture gradient information might be weighted more heavily than binocular disparities.

In summary, the perception of the 3-D world may not be as problematic as has often been assumed. In fact, it could be argued that we are particularly fortunate because there are multiple sources of information to tell us about the different aspects of the 3-D structure of objects—their depths, distances, and shapes and their layout in the world. The fact that the retina is a 2-D surface is irrelevant—the availability of information is the key to understanding how we see the structure and layout of the surrounding world, as it is for all aspects of perception. It is easy to think that extracting information about 2-D shape is less problematic because there is 'a shape' in the image on the retina but this is misleading. Judging the 2-D shapes of objects in the world is a 3-D task. Similarly, flatness is a 3-D property of surfaces, not some default state as a consequence of having a 2-D image.

Chapter 6
Perception and action

Background

Traditionally, we have thought of the different senses as providing input information about the world we live in and that our conscious perceptions (*qualia*) are the output of our perceptual processes. It has also been assumed that we have separate attentional processes to select between the competing aspects of the perceptual information and these are followed by cognitive processes that give meaning to the sensory information. But think about it. The only reason why animals have evolved mechanisms to detect and pick up sensory information is that the information provides a selective advantage for the animal. In other words, perceptual processes have not evolved just to provide us with delightful (or not so delightful) *qualia* of the world but rather to allow us to act appropriately. Perception and action go together—a perceptual system by itself would be useless without an action system and an action system would be useless without a perceptual system. In 1966, James Gibson captured this idea very elegantly in the title of his book *The Senses Considered as Perceptual Systems*. Nowadays, few would disagree with the idea of a strong link between the extraction of sensory information and the control of action but there are many who see the perception–action function as only one of two possible functions of the human perceptual system—the other being the identification of objects and our conscious perception of the world. Support for this dual-route model of perceptual processing has come from physiological evidence of two distinct neural pathways, referred to as the dorsal and ventral streams, and this will be discussed in greater detail in Chapter 8.

The strong link between perception and action has been revealed in a variety of relatively low-level tasks such as helping us to maintain balance; providing information about our movements within the world (self-motion); allowing us to determine our direction of travel (heading); and helping us to estimate the time before we reach objects in the surrounding world (time-to-contact).

Maintenance of balance

In the past, it has been assumed that the most important source of information for maintaining our balance and posture comes from the vestibular system in the inner ear. We know that the otoliths and semicircular canals in the inner ear signal the linear acceleration and the rotation of our heads respectively. When we sway, these signals are used to control the muscles in our legs in order to minimize that sway and thereby maintain our balance and stable posture. In the 1970s, David Lee pointed out that body sway also produces optic flow when there are surfaces in the surrounding environment that are not too distant from the observer. The easiest way to think about the optic flow that results from body sway is to imagine an array of strings from various points in the surrounding (stationary) world that all converge at the eyeball (Figure 30(a)). As long as the distances are not too great, those strings will change their directions in a very lawful way during each movement of the observer. This is optic flow.

To study the effect of optic flow on balance, Lee built a suspended room consisting of three walls and a ceiling that could swing back and forth through a few centimetres around the observer—the

(a)

(b)

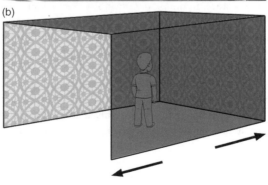

swinging room (Figure 30(b)). As a consequence, the pattern of optic flow at the observer's eye is similar to that produced by the natural swaying movements of the observer—an expanding pattern as the room moves toward the observer (Figure 6(b)) and a contracting pattern as the room moves away. He found that observers swayed in time with the small sinusoidal movements of the room and he described his observers as being 'hooked like puppets'. This result provides strong evidence that we use optic flow information to control our muscles and correct our posture. The desired goal is to minimize the optic flow because this would (normally) indicate that the observer was not moving or swaying. Although Lee's results provide strong evidence for the role of optic flow in the maintenance of balance, this is not to say that vestibular information is not also used. For example, we are able to maintain balance even in the dark, but clearly optic flow can be a very useful source of information when it is available.

Once again, it is useful to consider the particular environment in which we have evolved. We are terrestrial creatures which means that the ground plane surface under our feet always creates optic flow when we move. It follows that optic flow would not be a reliable source of information for birds that fly more than a few metres off the ground because at a greater distance there would be little or no optic flow. Hence, it should not surprise us to discover that birds of prey rely more on vestibular signals as a source of information about their own posture and movements across the sky than on optic flow.

One of the striking findings of Lee's experiments with the swinging room is that observers are typically unaware that they

30. (a) The idea of an optic array is captured in this shop window display. The strings from different objects in the world all converge at a particular vantage point. When the vantage point moves, the directions of the strings change to create an optic flow pattern. (b) David Lee's swinging room. When the suspended room moves back and forth, the observer sways back and forth in synchrony.

are swaying—the use of optic flow to control body posture occurs quite unconsciously. However, if the amplitude and/or velocity of the room movement is increased, observers report that they feel they are moving in the opposite direction to the room's motion. This experience of self-motion is referred to as ego-motion or vection. As with balance, the optic flow produced by the swinging room provides information that the observer is moving in the opposite direction to the room's movement, but note that the perception of self-motion from optic flow contradicts the vestibular signals that the observer is not moving. It could be argued that the conflicting vestibular information is only weak (or absent) when the observer is actually stationary and therefore it is not too surprising that the optic flow information dominates our perceptual experience. To see whether this is true, Lee created a scenario in which the observer took a couple of steps forward (thereby generating strong vestibular signals) but her/his forward movements resulted in the suspended room moving forwards at twice the rate, in the *same* direction as the observer's movements. In this case, the optic flow from the room signalled that the observer was moving backwards, in the opposite direction. And this is what observers reported. Although they knew they were stepping forwards, they felt that they were moving backwards. This result provides clear evidence that the optic flow can override vestibular information in our perception of self-motion.

Vection and the elevator illusion

In the 1990s, Gunnar Johansson reported the results of another self-motion experiment that used two TV screens on either side of the observer's head to display a pattern of stripes moving upwards (or downwards) in the observer's peripheral vision. Even though the TV screens filled only a small portion of the entire visual field (unlike Lee's swinging room), most observers reported that they felt themselves to be moving downwards (or upwards)—that is, in the opposite direction to the pattern motion. The effect is referred to as the 'elevator illusion' because it mimics the situation of standing in a moving elevator with windows on either side to reveal the world outside. Johansson argued that although the angular extent of the two moving patterns was very small, the movement stimulated the peripheral retina and this plays an important role in our perception of self-motion. Readers may have noticed a similar effect when sitting in a stationary railway carriage. Although the interior of the carriage fills most of the visual field (and is stationary), a train moving on an adjacent track and seen through a side window (in peripheral vision) frequently causes us to feel that we are moving.

In Johansson's elevator illusion, the optic flow provides information that is consistent with the linear translation (upwards or downwards) of the observer. This is not too surprising because we know that the otoliths in the inner ear only provide information about acceleration. In an actual elevator, the otoliths can only signal observer movement at the start and finish of the elevator's movement which means that the only information about our upward or downward movement at constant speed is given by optic flow. The situation is different when the observer *rotates* around one of the three principal axes—the z axis (roll), the x axis (pitch), and the y axis (yaw) (Figure 31(a)). In these cases, the semicircular canals in the inner ear provide continuous information about the observer's rotation. Consider the situation of a stationary observer who views a large disc directly in front of her/him covered with a random texture and rotating around the z (roll) axis. Observers typically report that they feel that they are rotating (rolling) in the opposite direction to the movement of the disc—another example of vection. This demonstrates that the optic flow created by the rotating disc is sufficient to produce the impression of observer rotation even when there is no confirmatory information from the semicircular canals. However, although most observers report that they feel they are rotating in the opposite direction to the disc initially, they rarely feel that they completely tumble through 360 degrees.

(a)

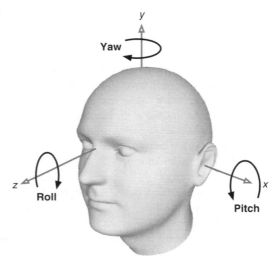

(b)

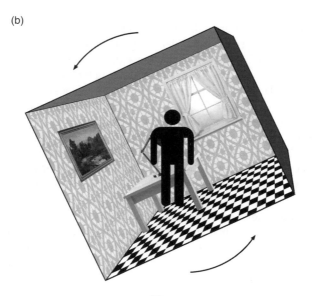

Perception

90

The tumbling room

To establish why observers rarely feel that they tumble through
360 degrees in a typical vection experiment, Ian Howard built
an entire cuboid room that could rotate around the straight
ahead (z) axis of the stationary observer. For the majority of
observers, he found that the room would induce a feeling of
continuous 'tumbling'—in the opposite direction to the room's
motion. Moreover, he found that the rotating room was more
likely to produce the impression of tumbling than a rotating
sphere covered with random dots that filled the entire visual field
and thereby generated maximum optic flow. Howard attributed
the more powerful effect in the rotating room to the room's
rectangular frame together with the presence of objects such as a
table top with objects resting on it that would normally signal
what is 'up' and 'down' in the world (Figure 31(b)). Seen together,
these results suggest that although optic flow plays a very
important role in determining our perception of self-motion,
others factors also play a role.

Direction of heading

When we walk or run across a ground plane surface, the optic
flow created by our movements provides information not only
that we are moving but also about the direction in which we are
travelling—the so-called 'direction of heading'. In his 1950
book—*The Perception of the Visual World*—Gibson illustrated this
with a figure showing the optic flow that would be created when
an aircraft approaches a runway (Figure 32(a)). He pointed out
that the focus of expansion in the optic array—the point at the

31. **(a) The three axes of rotation—roll, pitch, and yaw. (b) An
impression of Ian Howard's tumbling room that rotates around the
straight-ahead (z) axis of the stationary observer. The observer
perceives him-/herself to be tumbling in the opposite direction
especially when the room contains objects that would normally
indicate 'up' and 'down' in the world.**

32. (a) The outwards optic flow created by an aircraft that is about to land. (b) The focus of expansion in the optic flow field for a bird flying over land is in the direction of travel.

centre of the outward flow of motion—signals the instantaneous direction of travel (Figure 32(b)). The situation is slightly more complicated if we consider what happens on the retina rather than the optic array because the observer is always able to direct her or his gaze to a point in the visual field and thereby cancel out that point's motion. As a consequence, it seems likely that we have to use additional information about the movements of the eyes in order to recover the actual direction of heading.

Experiments have shown that walking observers are able to judge their direction of heading with a precision close to 1 degree of visual angle but this does not prove that optic flow information is being used. In addition to optic flow, there are proprioceptive signals indicating the position of the eye in the head and the position of the head on the shoulders. These signals provide information about the *visual direction* of a particular target with respect to our bodies (the target's ego-centric direction) and hence this information could be used to orient our bodies in the direction of the desired locomotion. Note that unlike optic flow, visual direction information can be used by a stationary as well as a moving observer.

How can we tell which source of information—optic flow or visual direction—is used when we are asked to walk towards a visual target? A simple wedge-shaped displacing prism, positioned just in front of the observer's eye, has the effect of displacing the entire visual field to one side or, more correctly, of causing the observer's eye to rotate to a different position when viewing a particular target. Hence, visual direction information from proprioceptive signals of the eye with respect to the head, and the head with respect to the body, is altered and this should result in the observer walking in the displaced visual direction, if proprioceptive signals are used. On the other hand, displacing prisms do not alter the characteristics of the expanding flow field and its focus. If optic flow information is used to guide walking, this will result in the observer walking in the correct direction towards the target. As a consequence, this paradigm provides a useful way of separating out the effects of the two sources of information.

Experimental findings from Simon Rushton and Bill Warren show that walking paths are displaced away from the direction of the target, as would be expected if the observer were using proprioceptive information, but often not to the full extent of the prismatic displacement. This suggests that we make use of both sources of information and the source of information that is most influential depends on the particular conditions such as the speed of movement of the observer and the characteristics of the surrounding environment. Gibson himself described how he would sometimes turn to face backwards while driving his car and, in response to his wife's protestations, he pointed out that he knew where he was going without having to look in that direction! Gibson's logic was that the contracting visual field created while looking backwards (Figure 32(b)) contained equally valid information about the car's direction of travel.

Time-to-contact

As we move through the visual world, the optic flow field expands outwards from a central point (Figure 32(b)) and simple geometry reveals that the rate of expansion of the flow field provides information about the time before we reach some place in the surrounding world, if we are moving at a constant speed. The astronomer Fred Hoyle was the first to notice that the inverse of the rate of angular expansion (1/rate of dilation) created by an object approaching us at a constant velocity specified the time in seconds before that object will reach us—this is referred to as the *time-to-contact*. This idea was taken up by David Lee in the context of human perceptual abilities and is referred to as the τ (tau) hypothesis (Figure 33). The idea is attractive because it suggests that we should be able to judge when an approaching object, such as a ball, will reach us and hence we will have time to initiate the appropriate finger movements (in advance) in order to catch that ball successfully. Ball catching, like many other visually guided tasks, has to be based on timing information. The τ strategy can be contrasted with the traditional view in which it is assumed that timing judgements (t) are based on an estimate of the distance (d) to the ball and an estimate of its approach velocity

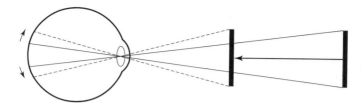

33. Time-to-contact. As an object approaches the observer, the image on the retina dilates (expands) and geometry shows that the inverse of the rate of dilation—τ—specifies the time before the object will reach the observer.

(v) ($v = d/t \therefore t = d/v$). However, if we were able to use the rate of dilation of the flow field created by the approaching ball, this would provide us with a direct estimate of the time-to-contact that is independent of both distance and velocity.

Crossing a busy road provides a rather practical example of the potential usefulness of a τ strategy. Given that it takes a particular amount of time to cross a road, it would be useful to be able to detect the time remaining before an approaching car would reach the road crossing and this is given directly by τ. Moreover, this estimate is independent of how far away the car is and its speed. This logic led to one of Lee's research projects that aimed to teach young children how to cross a road safely. The time-to-contact information provided by the rate of dilation was also one of the factors that led car manufacturers to include a third light in the braking lights of cars on the grounds that it would allow drivers to judge more accurately whether, and how quickly, they were catching up with the car in front.

So far we have considered the computational theory of time-to-contact information, but is there any evidence that it is used by the human visual system? In an experiment using experienced long jumpers, Lee showed that in running up to the take-off board, long jumpers do not rely on a standardized and highly practised run-up (as the jumpers themselves believed) but instead they adjust their stride length just before the take-off point. Lee proposed that the information they used to adjust those last few strides in order to land precisely on the take-off board was based on time-to-contact information. He argued that the variable the athletes could control in the run-up to the board was the upward force exerted by the leg and this would determine the time that the athlete was in the air on each stride. Using the rate of dilation to estimate the remaining time before reaching the take-off board would allow the long jumper to adjust the upward force and thus the timing of the remaining strides in order to reach the correct take-off point for the long jump. There is also evidence that many other species, including humming birds, gannets, and pigeons, are able to use a τ strategy.

Affordances

The examples discussed in this chapter so far have revealed the importance of optic flow information in the control of action and the close link between perception and action. However, the tasks involved—balance, self-motion, direction of heading, and time-to-contact—might be considered to be relatively 'low-level' aspects of the perception–action system. Gibson's view of perception went much further and he suggested that the 'meaning' of the sensory information was the essence of why we have perceptual processes in the first place. It is important to remember that this is not meaning in a cognitive sense—something we use language to think and talk about—but rather meaning in the sense of what the world offers us or allows us to do. Gibson referred to this idea as the *affordances* of the world. For Gibson, the purpose of our perceptual systems is not to identify objects as objects, as Marr and others have assumed, but rather to extract information about what we might do with those objects and how we might respond to events in the world. Note that long before a young child develops language and the ability to recognize and name objects, she or he can act appropriately—for instance, hiding behind a desk or sofa.

The idea of affordances is new but its origins can be seen in the work of the Gestalt psychologist Kurt Koffka in the early 20th century, who talked about the *demand characteristics* of the world. To most ethologists, the idea that animals are able to detect the affordances of the world seems obvious—a bird can detect a suitable nesting place and appropriate food—but the idea that there could be 'meaning' in the patterns of light reaching our eyes (and the other senses) has been resisted by the majority of psychologists. In part, this may be due to the British philosophical tradition of empiricism and associationism that has emphasized the need to learn and to associate the meanings of the world with particular sensory states. It is, of course, an empirical question as to whether we have to learn about the affordances of the world or whether they are innately given but, irrespective of the answer to this question, there has to be something there in the pattern of light that tells us what the world offers. If there is sufficient information in the pattern of sensory stimulation to be associated with a particular past experience or meaning, there must be sufficient information to specify that particular state of the world. I find it curious that we are willing to accept that the disparities created by a particular surface can provide information about the shape of that surface but not what that surface offers us with respect to our potential actions.

Take, for example, the ground plane surface that we, as terrestrial creatures, walk over all the time. There are some surfaces that afford walking on and other surfaces, such as water, that do not. Clearly, there must be something different about the patterns of light reaching our eyes from solid surfaces that indicate they can be walked on from those produced by liquid surfaces, such as a lake or pond, that do not. Whether or not this has to be learned is not the question. There must be some invariant property of the pattern of light to indicate or specify whether the surface is solid or not. We can be fooled, of course. A pond covered with a thin layer of ice has many of the properties of a surface that can be walked on and this can mislead a young child into thinking that it is safe to walk on the ice. But our reluctance to walk on such a surface is not a result of perceptual information (which does not differentiate a thin and dangerous layer of ice from a thick and safe layer) but rather a consequence of our cognitive knowledge that results in the decision to override the perceptual information. And this is what we teach our children.

Although the logical arguments for the use of affordances seem compelling, is there any evidence that affordances underlie human behaviour? The results of Eleanor Gibson's visual cliff experiment are very suggestive. There is a story that when Eleanor Gibson was with her young children visiting the Grand Canyon, she wondered what it was that prevented her children from straying over the cliff edge. However, it turns out that this trip was not the inspiration for her later experiments using the apparatus known as the *visual cliff* in which there is a sudden drop of a couple of feet from an upper platform to a lower surface (Figure 34). In those experiments, she placed young infants on the upper platform to see whether they would crawl over the visual cliff. (The entire apparatus was covered with a glass sheet so there was no possibility that the infant would fall.) She found that infants never strayed over the visual cliff even when they were encouraged to do so by their carers. The results of her experiment have often been interpreted as showing that infants can detect the depth and distance at that early age but this misses the point. It seems more likely that the infants avoid crawling over the cliff because the visual information specifies an affordance—danger.

Biological motion

Traditional approaches to the study of perception have focused on the information that is available in a single snapshot of the world—the colours, the contours, and the depth and distance. However, as Gibson and others have pointed out, this leaves out the vast amount of information that is available in the changing patterns of light and dark that reach our eyes. One particular

34. Gibson and Walk's visual cliff. Young infants typically do not stray over the deep side of the cliff even though there is a sheet of glass to prevent them from falling.

aspect of this dynamic information has been the focus of much research in recent years—*biological motion*—the patterns of motion created by moving animals. In the early 1970s, Gunnar Johansson produced a series of movies that depicted people undertaking a variety of actions such as walking, dancing, and running. In Johansson's movies, however, the only information about the walker's movements was provided by the complex patterns of motion of a small number of point-lights attached to the joints between the walker's limbs and body (Figure 35). The point-lights in any single frame of the movie appear as a random collection of dots, but when observers view the movie sequence, they are able to judge not only the particular actions undertaken—walking, running, or dancing—but also the gender of the walker or dancer, their age, and in some cases even their identity, if the walker is a close friend. In stimulus terms, Johansson's point-light displays might be described as impoverished compared with what is normally present but his displays clearly capture the rich information that is available in the patterns of relative motion.

Using similar point-light displays, Sverker Runeson and Gunilla Frykholm showed that observers are also able to accurately judge the weight of a box lifted by an actor when there were just 21 point-lights on the actor and the box. Differing views have emerged as to what the critical information might be in these point-light displays—the movements of the end-points of rigid structures such as the limbs or the characteristic patterns of

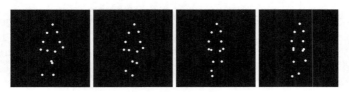

35. **A sequence of images in a point-light display of an individual walking.**

motion in the wrists and ankles—but all investigators agree that there is rich information in these complex patterns of motion.

Causality

One of the first attempts to identify the visual information specifying the 'meaning' of events in the surrounding world was carried out by Albert Michotte in the 1940s. He was interested in the information that specified causality—when the action of one object causes an action in a second object. He constructed a simple display depicting a square that moved across a screen at a constant speed before reaching a second, stationary square. At the moment of 'impact', the first square stopped moving and the second square started moving in the same direction as the first. When the temporal and spatial conditions were just right, observers reported seeing the first square 'colliding' and 'pushing' the second square along the same trajectory. Timing was crucial to obtain this percept. If there was a short delay before the second square started moving or the second square started moving before the 'impact' of the first square, the impression of causation was abolished. Michotte claimed that the perception of causality was a direct process and didn't involve higher-level expectations or cognitive influences. This idea is very appealing and there is now evidence that six-month-old infants are able to perceive causality in displays similar to those used by Michotte.

One of the reasons why some vision scientists find it difficult to accept that perceptual processes could be 'direct' and not susceptible to higher-level influences is the apparent complexity of the computations that are necessary to extract perceptual information (cf. Marr's comments about the complexity of the information processing problems). To counter this view, Runeson proposed the idea of a *smart perceptual mechanism* that could provide 'direct' information without calculation or computation. He cited the 'polar planimeter' as a practical example. This is a device that can measure the area of a 2-D patch by moving a stylus around the circumference of the patch. Area is not computed by measuring area in the usual way—length times breadth—but is given directly by the output of the device. Gibson himself used the metaphor of resonance. Consider a device like a radio receiver. A radio does not 'process information' but rather its circuits resonate, with appropriate tuning, to the frequencies of different radio stations. For the human perceptual system, Gibson argued we have 'attuned' perceptual mechanisms that resonate to the available information in the world.

Present-day neural network or *connectionist* models provide a better metaphor for thinking about perceptual processes than the resonance of radio receivers. Connectionist models can be taught a task such as face recognition using feedback to modify the weights of the connections between hypothetical 'neurons'. As a result of the learning, these models are capable of differentiating and identifying different faces, not by storing representations of those faces, but by setting up differently attuned neural structures that could be thought of as resonating to particular facial images. As a consequence, learning can be thought of as a process of attunement and differentiation rather than the laying down of memories. But although Gibson was right in emphasizing the richness of the information that is available in the world, he had much less to say about the nature of the attuned mechanisms that are needed to pick up that information.

Chapter 7
Delusions about illusions

The term illusion is used to describe situations where we make mistakes and perceive the surrounding world incorrectly. For the indirect theorists, illusions provide strong evidence that our perceptions are not direct but depend instead on assumptions, inferences, hypotheses, and other 'higher-level' processes. But what is an illusion? Richard Gregory described illusions as 'departures from reality' and this fits with our everyday idea that illusions represent situations where what we perceive does not correspond to some physical characteristic of the particular scene. In the Müller-Lyer illusion, for example, we see the upper horizontal line (with the outgoing fins) as longer than the lower line (with the ingoing fins) despite the fact that they are, in reality, exactly the same length (Figure 36(a)). In the Ebbinghaus illusion (Figure 36(b)), the circle on the right (surrounded by the smaller circles) appears to be larger than the same-sized circle on the left that is surrounded by larger circles. In both illusions, the size we perceive does not correspond to the real size, as can be verified by using a ruler or tape measure.

Explanations of illusions

The Müller-Lyer and Ebbinghaus illusions are typically referred to as geometric illusions along with the Ponzo, Hering, Poggendorf, Zöllner, Café Wall, and Fraser illusions (Figure 37). There have

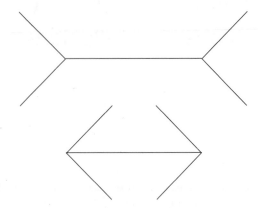

(b)

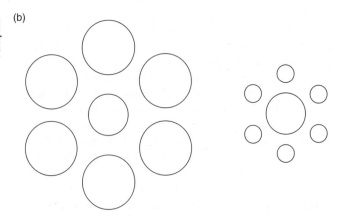

36. (a) The upper line in the Müller-Lyer illusion appears to be longer than the lower line although they are the same length. (b) The right-hand centre circle appears to be larger than the left-hand centre circle in the Ebbinghaus illusion although they are the same size.

been many attempts to explain and classify our incorrect perceptions in terms of either low-level mechanisms such as inhibition, or higher-level 'cognitive' processes such as inappropriate size scaling. Jim Robinson classified illusions with respect to similarities in the type of distortion caused by the illusory figure—distortions of length, angle, size, movement, and so on. Richard Gregory, on the other hand, classified illusions according to their cause—which might be either 'physical', 'physiological', or 'cognitive'. Terminology is very important for understanding the illusion concept and my preference is to limit the word illusion to those situations where we incorrectly perceive the world as a consequence of the characteristics of our perceptual systems. Hence, I do not regard rainbows, mirages, doppler shifts in frequency, and moiré patterns as illusions because they are consequences of the physics of the world. As such, they exist independently of any perceptual system. They are interesting effects that can be explained by the laws of physics but they should not be regarded as illusions.

Illusions that have a 'physiological basis'

Let us consider first those perceptual effects that are thought to be consequences of the underlying mechanisms. There are two main classes: (i) successive contrast effects (or after-effects) that are the result of sustained sensory stimulation and (ii) simultaneous contrast effects (or induced effects) that are the result of influences from neighbouring stimuli. For successive contrast effects, we know that nearly all sensory systems adapt as a result of sustained stimulation. As a consequence, we experience after-effects such as after-images, the motion after-effect (waterfall illusion), size and spatial frequency after-effects. John Frisby has described these after-effects as 'the psychologist's micro-electrode' because they have the potential to reveal the properties of the underlying mechanisms.

We also know that neighbouring stimuli can affect perceptual appearance—simultaneous contrast effects. The identical grey squares in Figure 38(a) appear to be different—the square surrounded by the light area appears darker than the same square

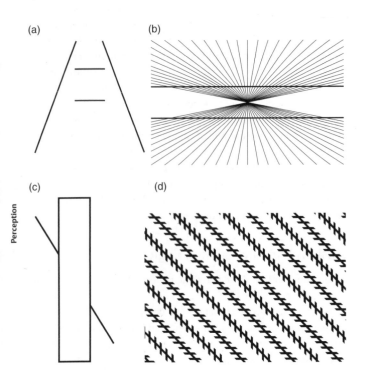

37. Examples of the (a) Ponzo, (b) Hering, (c) Poggendorf, (d) Zöllner, (e) Café Wall, and (f) Fraser illusions. In the Ponzo illusion, the upper horizontal line appears to be longer than the lower line even though they are the same length. The two horizontal lines in the Hering illusion are actually straight but they appear to be curved. The two parts of the diagonal line in the Poggendorf illusion appear be misaligned although they are physically aligned. In the Zöllner illusion, the diagonal lines are actually parallel although they do not appear to be. The horizontal lines in the Café Wall illusion appear to converge and diverge although they are actually parallel. In the Fraser spiral, the apparently spiralling contours are actually circles.

(e)

(f)

37. Continued.

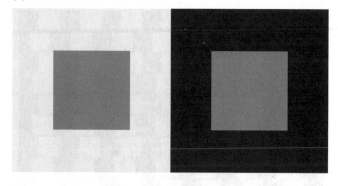

Perception

38. Two examples of simultaneous contrast. (a) The left-hand grey square appears darker than the right-hand square although they are the same grey. (b) Each of the vertical bars is the same grey but they look very different when superimposed on the light-to-dark gradient of the background.

surrounded by a dark area. This is simultaneous lightness contrast. In the motion domain, the moon appears to move in the opposite direction to the movement of the clouds across its surface—this is induced motion. The Hering and Zöllner illusions in Figure 37 have been explained in terms of simultaneous contrast (inhibition) between orientation detectors.

Illusions that have a 'cognitive basis'

How should we understand Richard Gregory's third class of illusions—illusions that have a 'cognitive' rather than a 'physiological' basis? What might this mean? According to Gregory, the figure–ground effects seen in Rubin's vase and the reversals in the Necker cube have a 'cognitive' basis (Figure 39). These are ambiguous figures and, in both cases, our perception

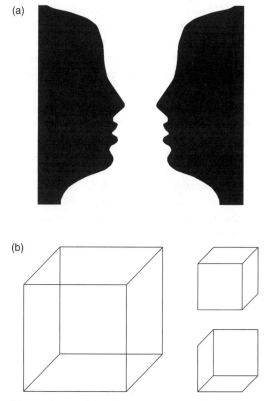

(a)

(b)

39. Ambiguous figures: (a) Rubin's vase, and (b) the Necker cube.

alternates between the two different possibilities—we see the Rubin's figure as a white vase or two black faces depending on whether the white or dark area is seen as the figure rather than the background. A particular face of the Necker cube can be seen as in front or behind and our perception alternates spontaneously between these two possibilities depicted on the right.

Gregory referred to the alternative perceptions as 'perceptual hypotheses' and he proposed that we 'choose' between the two possibilities. The idea of choosing certainly suggests the involvement of higher-level cognitive processes. But does this follow? Could the perceptual alternation be due to some relatively low-level process of fatigue or adaptation rather than choosing between hypotheses? In my view, 'choosing' seems more of a description of what happens, rather than an explanation.

At present, there is little consensus on how we should account for these perceptual alternations but we might agree that the alternations are often a consequence of the insufficiency of the available information. If the faces of the Necker cube are opaque, rather than outline drawings (Figure 39b, far right), the ambiguity goes away. If there is disparity information to indicate that the vase part of the Rubin's figure lies in front of the surrounding area, the ambiguity goes away. This suggests that these particular 'cognitive' illusions may be limited to rather artificial or impoverished stimulus situations.

When is an illusion not an illusion?

We know from classroom demonstrations, as well as controlled experiments, that nearly all observers are susceptible to the illusions just described. In other words, there is general agreement about what we perceive in these illusory situations—for example the Müller-Lyer figure with outgoing fins looks longer than the figure with the ingoing fins. What is less obvious is how we should define the thing we call 'reality'. Is there a single physical reality that can be used to describe the input to our perceptual systems? The answer is no—there can be many different descriptions of the physical reality. The characteristics of the retinal image represent one possible reality—psychologists refer to it as the 'proximal stimulus'. Based on this definition of 'reality', the Müller-Lyer and the Ebbinghaus figures (Figure 36) would both be classified as illusions because we perceive the figures as different despite the fact that the retinal sizes of the Müller-Lyer lines or Ebbinghaus circles are the same.

But what about the desktop in front of me? The retinal image of my desktop is trapezoidal in shape (because I am viewing its rectangular surface obliquely) so if the retinal shape is considered to be the 'reality' then my perception of the desktop as rectangular suggests that my perception should be classified as illusory. Similarly, if I perceive the heights of two same-sized individuals standing at different distances from me as the same, this should be regarded as an illusion because the retinal sizes of the two individuals are quite different. However, it doesn't make sense to describe the perception of my desk as rectangular and the perception of the two individuals as the same height as illusions because what we perceive is consistent with the real-world properties of the desk and the heights of the individuals. The retinal shape and size represent one particular description of reality and the real-world size and shape represent a different description of the reality.

The same argument applies to all the so-called 'constancies' of our perceptual systems—we perceive the size, shape, lightness, depth, and colour of objects and surfaces in the world as being the same (i.e. more or less constant) despite the fact that the retinal image properties can be very different. It follows that the size, shape, luminance, disparity, and wavelength characteristics of the retinal image are probably not the most appropriate descriptions of the physical 'reality' if we are trying to determine whether our perceptions are veridical or illusory. Helmholtz made this point 150 years ago when he wrote:

> I am myself disposed to think that neither the size, form and position of the real retina nor the distortions of the image projected on it matter at all...

Proximal and distal stimuli

The preceding discussion suggests that the 'proximal' stimulus may not be the most appropriate description of 'reality' and that the properties of objects in the world—the so-called 'distal' stimulus—might be a better description of 'reality'. My desktop is rectangular and what I perceive is a rectangular-shaped desk and hence there is nothing illusory about my perception. Although this definition sounds much better, there are still problems. Take, for example, the famous Ames Room (Figure 1). The Ames Room is not a normal rectangular room but instead it is trapezoidal in shape with the far left corner much further away than the right corner. The secret of the Ames Room is that it is constructed so that the back wall increases in height as it recedes off to the far left corner and thereby creates the same pattern of light at the eye as a normal, rectangular room (Figure 40(a)). For this to be true, the room has to be viewed from one particular vantage point, with just one eye to eliminate the binocular disparities, and with the observer stationary in order to eliminate the motion parallax information that might reveal its true shape. Should the Ames Room be considered to be an illusion? The argument in favour is that what we perceive—a normal rectangular room—does not correspond to the 'distal' stimulus—the 'real', trapezoidal shape of the room—and hence it should to be regarded as an illusion.

Projectively equivalent situations

But does this make any sense? In order to 'fool' the visual system, the Ames Room has to be carefully constructed so that the pattern of light reaching the eye is exactly the same as that created by a normal rectangular room. If this is done successfully, then no seeing machine—biological or man-made—could tell the difference and hence our 'illusory' perception cannot tell us anything about the human visual system. The more appropriate question to ask is why we perceive both an Ames Room and a normal, rectangular room as rectangular. The answer can be found in the perspective information that is present in both cases. The boundaries between the rear wall and the floor and ceiling are parallel, the shapes of the windows are rectangular and their frames have a constant thickness, and the gradient of the texture on the rear wall is even (Figure 40(a)). All these characteristics provide information that the back wall lies in a frontal rather than a slanting plane. Hence, as Richard Gregory pointed out:

> It must look like a normal room if constructed to strict perspective, and viewed from the right position, because the image it creates is the same as for an ordinary room.

This suggests that the Ames Room, by itself, is a rather trivial demonstration and tells us nothing that we could not have learned from looking at our perception of normal rooms. It is irrelevant that the shape of the room is trapezoidal because there is no information to tell us that the room is trapezoidal. If this argument is accepted, the Ames Room raises a more general issue. If the pattern of light reaching the eye (or eyes) from some artificially constructed scene is exactly the same as that created by some real-world situation, the artificially constructed scene cannot possibly tell us anything about our visual system that could not have been discovered by looking at the real-world situation it mimics. There are many other examples of 'projectively equivalent' situations that create exactly the same (or a very similar) pattern(s) of light to the eye(s). These include the viewing of images in a stereoscope (Figure 41).

(a)

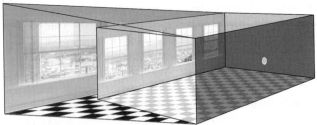

(b)

40. (a) An Ames Room is constructed so that the pattern of light
created by the trapezoidal room is the same as would be created by a
normal rectangular room when viewed from a particular peephole.
(b) This may look like an Ames Room but it is actually a normal,
rectangular room with two superimposed figures of different sizes.
The pattern of light reaching the eye from this normal room and the
two figures is the same as would be created by a real Ames Room
(Figure 1).

41. A stereoscope of the type designed by Oliver Wendell Holmes that uses prismatic lenses in front of the two eyes to view the two separate stereo pictures. The pictures themselves are flat but we see the scene in depth when the pictures are viewed through the stereoscope.

The physical reality of a pair of stereoscopic images is that the pictures themselves are flat but we see vivid depth when they are viewed through an appropriate device. Does that make our perception of the depth in a stereoscope illusory? I would argue that our perception is not illusory because the patterns of light reaching the two eyes are very similar to those that would be created if we were to view a real 3-D scene. If you are not convinced, imagine the situation of viewing the world through some virtual reality system with two small screens positioned just in front of the eyes which are fed with the signals from two cameras located just in front of the screens. Is the depth we see an illusion because the images on the screens are flat? Or is it not an illusion because what we see is consistent with the world just beyond the cameras? What is common to the viewing of a real world and the viewing of images in a stereoscope is that both situations create binocular disparities and these provide information about the 3-D structure and layout of the surrounding world, and this is what we perceive.

A similar argument can be made for other situations where the pattern of light reaching the eye is a copy or facsimile of some real-world situation. One of my favourite examples is Kokichi Sugihara's 'defying gravity' illusion (Figure 42(a)). Viewed from one particular vantage point, we perceive a collection of four ramps that appear to be slanted upwards to converge at a central platform. Nothing remarkable in that except that when a ball is placed at the 'bottom' of one of the ramps, it glides up the slanted ramp apparently defying gravity. How could this be possible? When the display is rotated around its centre or the viewer looks at the display from another vantage point (Figure 42(b)), the true 'reality' becomes apparent. The ramps are actually slanting downwards, not upwards, which accounts for the movement of the balls towards the central platform. The trick that Sugihara has employed so effectively is to create the appropriate perspective information to indicate the upward slopes of the ramps when

(a)   (b)

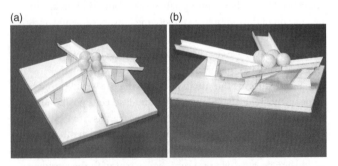

42. (a) Sugihara's 'defying gravity' illusion and (b) the same scene viewed from a different direction showing that the ramps are actually sloping downwards towards the central platform rather than upwards as they appear in (a).

the scene is viewed from one particular vantage point. Note also that we continue to be fooled even when we know what is happening.

Sugihara's demonstration won second prize in the 2013 *Illusion of the Year* competition but is it really an illusion? What we perceive from the original vantage point is perfectly consistent with the perspective information telling us about the 3-D structure of the situation and, once again, the trick involves creating a projectively equivalent stimulus that corresponds to another real-world scene. The important question raised by this demonstration is not whether it is an illusion but rather what are the perspective features of the display (and the real-world scene it mimics) that are responsible for our (mis)perception, and this is what interests Sugihara.

If the physical reality of these three situations—the trapezoidal shape of the Ames Room, the flatness of stereoscopic images, and the actual structure of Sugihara's display—should not be regarded as the appropriate basis for judging the correctness of our perceptions, what is the alternative? The answer seems to be that we need to consider the *information* these situations provide. There is perspective information in the case of both the Ames Room and Sugihara's display and disparity information in the case of the stereoscopic images. In all three cases, what we perceive is consistent with the information provided and therefore I would argue that it is inappropriate to regard these three situations as illusions. It follows that a better definition of what constitutes an illusion might be when there is a discrepancy between the available information and what we perceive. Hence, the available 'information' becomes the 'objective or physical reality'.

Information as the 'reality'

If information is the reality, how should we define 'information'? Take, for example, perspective information. Perspective is the name given to the projective characteristics of the world from a particular vantage point. For example, the angular size of identical objects varies inversely with their distance—Euclid's law. But note that there are many different properties of the perspective projections of the world we live in—parallel lines converge, surfaces create size and texture gradients, and there are gradients of foreshortening (width-to-height ratios) (Figure 21). Which particular aspect of perspective does the human visual system use? The answer might be all, but note that what constitutes information for a perceptual system becomes an empirical question about how our perceptual system actually works, rather than something derived from geometry.

If this is the case, there can't be any illusions because all of our perceptions are the consequences of the way our perceptual systems work. Thus, instead of being an objective description of the world and therefore the appropriate reference for deciding between correct and incorrect perception, the concept of *perceptual information* is necessarily a description of how our perceptual system actually works. 'Information' and 'how the system works' are two sides of the same coin. As discussed in Chapter 3, perceptual information is also species-specific, even though it is based on the properties of the physical world. The patterns of infra-red radiation emitted by warm-blooded creatures like ourselves provide information for snakes about our location but not for our own perceptual systems.

What I conclude from this is that there can be no meaningful distinction between the things that have been traditionally called illusions and the things that we regard as correct or veridical perceptions. This conclusion becomes clearer when one considers some other aspects of our perception that are not usually regarded as illusions but rather characteristics of 'how the system works'. Take thresholds, for example. If a dim light is not visible or a quiet tone is not heard, we do not conclude that these are visual or auditory illusions but rather consequences of how our perceptual systems work—that is, all sensory systems have thresholds. Similarly, we do not typically regard the fact that a metameric mixture of red and green light is seen as (and is indistinguishable from) yellow as an illusion—it is simply seen as a consequence of how our trichromatic visual system works. Finally, we do not regard our inability to see the very fine detail of objects far away from us as an illusion—it is just a consequence of our limited visual acuity.

What are the implications of this conclusion for the study of the things that have traditionally been called illusions? Are they no longer worth studying? I would argue that they are. These perceptual effects, as I prefer to call them, provide insights into how our perceptual systems work, but once we understand how and why a particular effect is created, for instance colour metamers, we no longer regard it as an illusion but just how that particular aspect of the perceptual system works. If this is true, it suggests that the only remaining 'illusions' are those aspects of perception that we don't yet understand!

There is, however, a potential problem in the search for 'illusions'. Many illusions, including the majority of the so-called geometrical illusions such as the Müller-Lyer and Ponzo, use simple line stimuli that are very impoverished in terms of the information they provide. The image of the pair of converging lines in Figure 43(a) could have been created by a pair of lines that actually converge in the plane of the page or a pair of parallel lines that recede into the distance. But note that the ambiguity only exists if the lines are thin. If they have thickness, like objects in the real world, the ambiguity disappears (Figure 43(b)). The important but unsurprising conclusion is that if you take away the information normally used by the visual system, our perceptual systems fail, and this tells us very little.

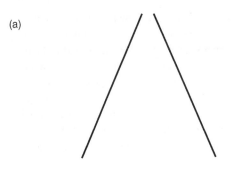

(a)

(b)

43. (a) A pair of thin, converging lines could have been created by a pair of parallel lines receding into the distance *or* a pair of converging lines in the plane of the page. (b) When the same lines have a thickness, the ambiguity goes away—they are seen as railway tracks disappearing into the distance.

Perceptual effects and invariant characteristics

Many previous attempts to classify illusions have missed the point that all our perceptions, and not just the so-called illusions, are dependent on the particular characteristics of the mechanisms we use to extract perceptual information. As a consequence, all perceptual effects (both veridical and illusory) have the potential to reveal the 'strategies' that are used to extract information for a range of different sensory attributes and in the different sensory modalities. What might those strategies be? It seems very likely that our perceptual systems have evolved to extract the invariant characteristics of the world—the things that don't change—rather than requiring mechanisms to 'correct' for things that do change. A good example can be found in the extraction of information about surface lightness and colour. The amount of light and the particular wavelengths reaching our eyes from a particular surface contain no information about the reflectance characteristics of that surface because they are always confounded by the effects of the illumination. On the other hand, the relative amounts of light reaching us from neighbouring surfaces have the potential to provide us with information about surface reflectance because they allow the confounding effects of the illumination to be discounted. Similarly, spatial comparisons can provide a way of discounting the confounding effects of distance on our ability to judge size and depth. Angular (or retinal) size provides no information about the size of objects in the world because angular size is always confounded by the distance from the observer. The relative size of similar objects, on the other hand, is invariant when those objects are seen against the texture of a receding ground plane (Figure 21).

Identifying the invariant features of the spatio-temporal pattern of light reaching our eyes is an important and promising strategy for trying to understand how our perceptual systems work. On the other hand, simplifying the characteristics of what is presented to observers may only tell us what happens when we take away the information that the perceptual system normally uses. This is why the use of impoverished stimuli, such as the typical illusion figures, doesn't necessarily tell us much about how our perceptual systems function normally.

Chapter 8
The physiology and anatomy of the visual system

Mechanism and process

The ways in which psychologists and physiologists use the terms 'mechanism' and 'process' are quite different. For physiologists, the idea of a mechanism is linked to the actions of individual neurons, neural pathways, and the ways in which the neurons are connected up. For psychologists, on the other hand, the term is typically used to describe the *processes* the neural circuits may carry out. For example, the idea of 'adaptation' (e.g. motion adaptation as the cause of the motion after-effect) does not refer to a specific neural process but refers instead to the 'black box' concept of a decrease in the response of a process as a result of continued stimulation. In other words, the concept of adaptation is independent of whether it occurs in neurons, electronic circuits, or hydraulic systems. For David Marr, this distinction corresponds to the difference between an explanation at an 'algorithmic' (or psychological) level and an explanation at a 'mechanism' level. The distinction is important because it can lead to misunderstandings. For example, it is sometimes claimed that neurons transmit 'information'. This is incorrect. Neurons relay all-or-none spikes along their axons—and the train of spikes may, or may not, convey information.

Psychological and physiological evidence

There is another important difference between psychological (behavioural) and physiological evidence. The results of a well-designed behavioural study can reveal the *whole-system* properties of a perceptual system whereas the recordings from individual neurons or even the beautiful images derived from functional magnetic resonance imaging (fMRI) studies can only tell us about the activity of neurons in a particular part of the nervous system. Colour perception provides a useful example to illustrate this difference. Thomas Young's experiments in the early 19th century on colour matching provide unequivocal evidence that colour vision is trichromatic (at least for most of us). This means that somewhere in the extraction of colour information there must be a limit or bottleneck of just three channels to convey colour information. My own students often assert that Bowmaker, Dartnall, and Mollon's pioneering experiments using micro-spectrophotometry (revealing that there are just three different types of cones in the primate retina) provided the first objective evidence of trichromacy. But objectivity is not the issue. Even if it had been found that there were more than three cone types, this would not refute or contradict the idea of trichromacy as a 'whole-system' property and thus an overall limitation on our ability to perceive colour.

In his book *Vision*, David Marr made the following observation:

> Modern neurophysiology has learned much about the operation of the individual nerve cell, but disconcertingly little about the meaning of the circuits that they compose in the brain.

In the remainder of the chapter, I shall attempt to provide a description of what we have learned from neurophysiology and anatomy over the past eighty years and what this tells us about the meaning of the circuits involved in the processing of visual information.

Limulus

The preceding remarks are general caveats about the differences between behavioural and physiological evidence but this is not to say that we have not learned a great deal about the physiological mechanisms and processes that underlie this thing we call perception. For example, the pioneering work of Keffer Hartline and Clarence Graham in 1932, recording from neurons in the horseshoe crab (Limulus), showed that the rate of firing in those neurons increases by ~20 spikes/s for every tenfold increase in the light reaching the Limulus eye (Figure 44). These results demonstrate that the intensity of light (like the intensity of sound and intensity in many other sensory dimensions) is coded logarithmically rather than linearly, at an early stage of processing. The link between psychological and physiological findings can be seen in the psychophysical observations made by Ernst Weber in the 19th century. He showed that the smallest 'just noticeable difference' (JND) between a stimulus and its background, that is, the threshold or ΔI, is typically proportional to the background level of the stimulus, I. For example, the amount of additional light that is needed to produce a just noticeable difference in the illumination of a scene increases with the background level of illumination: that is, ΔI is proportional to I and hence the ratio of ΔI to I is a constant: $\Delta I/I = k$. The constant k is known as the Weber fraction. Gustav Fechner later showed that the integration of Weber's equation predicts a logarithmic relationship between the perceived and the physical intensity of a stimulus $p = k \log (I)$, that is, the same relationship as Hartline and Graham observed in Limulus.

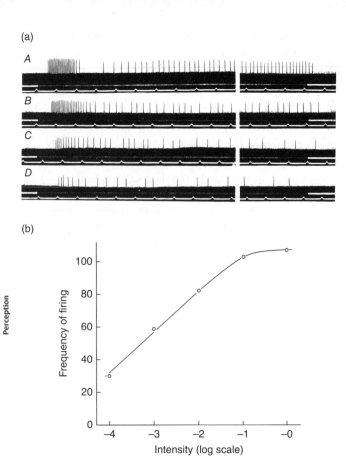

44. (a) Hartline and Graham's recordings from a single ommatidium in the horseshoe crab Limulus. The rate of firing is highest for the highest intensity of light falling on a particular ommatidium (top row) and decreases by ~ 20 spikes/s for every tenfold decrease in the amount of light (A→B→C→D). (b) The logarithmic relationship between the firing rate and the intensity of light can be seen when the frequency of firing is plotted against the logarithm of the intensity.

The retina

In the human retina, there are something like 120 million rod receptors and 6–8 million cone receptors. In contrast, there are only 1 million ganglion cells in the retina whose axons form the optic nerve leaving the eye (Figure 45). The fact that there are >100 times more receptors than ganglion cells suggests that we

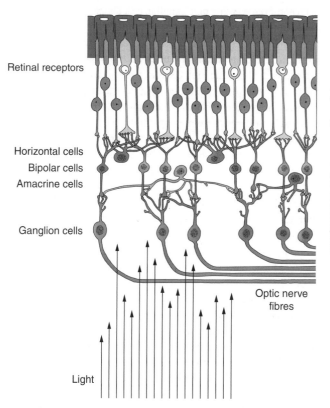

45. A schematic cross-section of the retina showing the retinal receptors, horizontal, bipolar, amacrine, and ganglion cells as well as the optic nerve fibres projecting from the retina to the LGN.

Retinal receptors

Horizontal cells
Bipolar cells
Amacrine cells

Ganglion cells

Optic nerve fibres

Light

must be losing out by having far fewer ganglion cells to convey information about the spatial patterns of light reaching our eyes. There is, however, an advantage in having multiple receptors converge onto each ganglion cell: adding or integrating the outputs of many receptors results in an increased sensitivity to light under conditions of poor illumination, albeit at the expense of poorer spatial resolution. In other words, there is a trade-off between sensitivity and spatial resolution: the greater the number of receptors converging on a ganglion cell, the greater the sensitivity but with the consequence of poorer spatial resolution. However, the human visual system has evolved a very clever way of dealing with this sensitivity–resolution trade-off. Physiological evidence has shown that the ganglion cells near the centre of the retina—in the fovea—receive an excitatory input from a single cone receptor whereas the ganglion cells in the periphery of the retina receive their excitatory inputs from many hundreds of rod receptors. As a consequence, our spatial acuity remains as good as it could be in foveal vision (at the expense of absolute sensitivity to light) while the absolute sensitivity to light is optimized in the peripheral retina (at the expense of spatial resolution). The lack of sensitivity to very dim targets in foveal vision is revealed if you look at a very dim star in the night sky. The star may be invisible when looked at directly but becomes visible when you turn your gaze slightly to one side, so that the star's image falls on receptors outside of the rod-free fovea.

We are usually quite unaware of the very poor spatial resolution in our peripheral vision until we try to resolve the fine detail of the surrounding scene. Once again, evolution has provided us with a solution—we don't need the whole of the retina to be high resolution because we can turn our eyes (and heads) to bring the parts of the surrounding world that previously stimulated the peripheral retina onto the high-resolution fovea.

So far, we have considered two aspects of early visual coding: the logarithmic transformation of stimulus energy into neural responses and the trade-off between sensitivity and spatial acuity in the peripheral and central areas of the retina. But how is the information about the spatial patterns of light falling on the retina coded in the visual system? In the human retina, the receptors synapse directly or indirectly with the bipolar, amacrine, and ganglion cells using continuous or graded responses (Figure 45). This is in contrast to the all-or-none spike trains that are relayed along the axons of the ganglion cells that form the optic nerve. Why should all-or-none spike trains be a feature of ganglion cells of the optic nerve (and most other neurons in the nervous system) rather than graded responses? The usual answer is that the electrical resistance of cell axons is very high and hence amplitude-modulated signals (like those driving a loudspeaker from an audio system) would become degraded very quickly if those signals had to be amplified multiple times along the length of an axon. A train of all-or-none spikes, on the other hand, can be faithfully transmitted and reproduced many times without degradation. Within the retina, however, the axon lengths are very short and therefore all-or-none spike trains are not necessary.

Lateral inhibition and receptive fields

The next question to ask is: what sort of information is coded in the patterns of neural activity that are sent along the optic nerve fibres from the ganglion cells to the visual cortex? The experiments carried out by Keffer Hartline and Floyd Ratliff on the horseshoe crab Limulus provide a clue. They recorded the signals from the axons connected to the individual ommatidia in the compound eye of Limulus. Not surprisingly, they found that an increase in the light falling on a particular ommatidium (A) increased the rate of firing in the associated axon (Figure 44). The surprising finding was that additional light falling on a neighbouring ommatidium (B) decreased the rate of firing of A—an effect referred to as *lateral inhibition* (Figure 46). As a consequence, the rate of firing in a particular axon signals the balance between the amount of light falling on a particular ommatidium and the

(a)

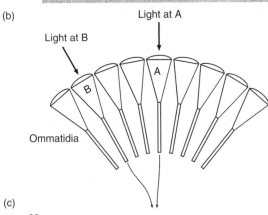

(b)

Light at B

Light at A

B

A

Ommatidia

(c)

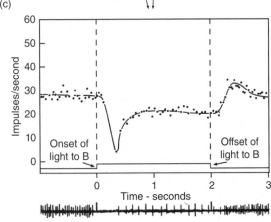

Onset of
light to B

Offset of
light to B

Time - seconds

130

amount of light falling on the immediately surrounding area. The total area of the receptors in the eye that affect the response of a single neuron is referred to as its *receptive field*.

Subsequent work by Horace Barlow and Stephen Kuffler showed that the ganglion cells in the mammalian retina have receptive fields with either on-centres and off-surrounds—excitation from receptors in the centre of the receptive field and inhibition from receptors in the surround of the receptive field (Figure 47(a))—or off-centres and on-surrounds with the opposite characteristics. In the 1960s, Robert Rodieck suggested that both the on-centre/off-surround and the off-centre/on-surround receptive fields could be modelled using two separate bell-shaped (or gaussian) distributions of receptors. For an on-centre/off-surround receptive field, the gaussian distribution (spread) of receptors that provides the excitatory input is much smaller than the gaussian distribution of receptors that provides the inhibitory input and vice versa for the off-centre/on-surround receptive fields (Figure 47(b)). Because the distributions of receptors providing both the excitatory and the inhibitory inputs are bell-shaped or gaussian, they are referred to as 'difference-of-gaussians' or DOG receptive fields.

So far, I have described the response characteristics of ganglion cells in the mammalian retina but the more interesting question is why the receptive fields might be 'wired-up' in this way. The first point to be made is that we shouldn't be surprised that the spatial patterns of light falling on the retina are not coded as a faithful 'picture' of the patterns of light coming from the surrounding world. Perception is about extracting information from those patterns of light rather than reproducing those patterns. In this respect, the purpose of perception is quite different from that of a

46. (a) The horseshoe crab Limulus. (b) A schematic diagram showing the effect of light falling on two different ommatidia in the Limulus eye. (c) The neural response showing how the onset of light to the second ommatidium (B) decreases the rate of firing in A—lateral inhibition.

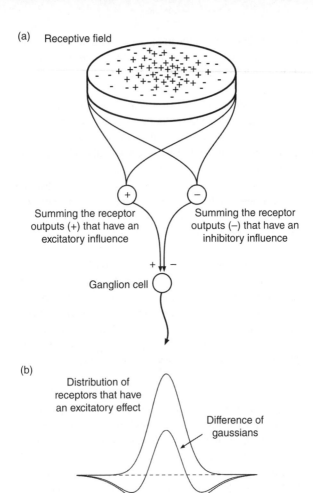

47. (a) A schematic diagram of an on-centre/off-surround receptive field. The + signs indicate receptors that have an excitatory influence on the ganglion cell's response and the – signs receptors that have an inhibitory influence. (b) Rodieck's modelling of the receptive field that involves excitatory influences from a narrower, gaussian distribution of receptors and inhibitory influences from a broader, gaussian distribution of receptors.

TV camera where the purpose is to reproduce the pattern of light reaching the camera as faithfully as possible (high fidelity) onto a TV screen. With this in mind, it is possible to see the role of the ganglion cell receptive fields as the first step in extracting information about the spatial changes of light: that is, the contours and boundaries of objects in the surrounding world. This interpretation is consistent with the observed responses of the ganglion cells. The largest responses are produced when the eye is stimulated with spatial changes of luminance—a simple spot of light on a dark background, a light/dark luminance edge, a pattern of light and dark stripes, a thin light line on a dark background, and so on. However, the exact 'role' or function of these receptive fields as components of a perceptual system is not a question that neurophysiological recordings can ever answer. We can speculate about the role of these receptive fields but we will never know for certain.

Feature detectors

It might be thought that the function of a particular cell could be established by determining the spatial pattern of light and dark that produces the largest response in that cell. For an on-centre/off-surround ganglion cell in the mammalian eye (Figure 47(a)), this would be a spot of light (of the correct size) on a dark background. Using this logic, we might think that the role or function of a ganglion cell was as a 'spot detector' because the largest response is produced by a spot of light. But a little thought shows that these cells could not possibly function as 'spot detectors', or any other sort of 'feature detector', because the response of a particular ganglion cell is necessarily *ambiguous*. Imagine that you could listen in to the rate of firing of a ganglion cell. A given rate of firing might be produced by a light spot on a dark background with a particular contrast and spot size. However, a similar rate of firing could also be produced by a light and dark grating pattern with the appropriate spacing between the light and dark bars with a different contrast, or a different colour, or a different size, or a slightly different position, or the corner of a light square on a dark background, and so on. The response of a particular cell by itself tells us almost nothing about the pattern of light and dark that was reaching that region of the retina other than it was some spatial patterning of light and dark rather than a homogeneous (uniform) distribution.

The response ambiguity means that the particular stimulus conditions that produce the best response in a cell may not tell us much about the function or role of that cell. For example, the locations of the peaks (best responses) in the spectral sensitivity curves for the different cone receptors in the retina—420, 535, and 565 nm—(Figure 12) are relatively unimportant because information about the spectral composition of the light reaching the receptors is provided by the pattern of activity over the different cone receptors. This point is important to bear in mind because the traditional strategy in neurophysiology has been to establish the spatio-temporal pattern of light and dark that produces the *largest* response for each of the cells studied.

The ambiguity in the response of a single ganglion cell in the mammalian retina means that these cells are not able to function as any sort of unique 'feature detector'. However, all is not lost because the activity of the hundreds, if not thousands, of ganglion cells that have their receptive fields in the same region of the retina will contain sufficient information about the pattern of light reaching the retina. Coding based on the activity of many neurons is referred to as *distributed* or *ensemble coding*. But note that the same consideration applies to the responses of neurons at all levels of the visual system: the response of any particular visual neuron is necessarily ambiguous with respect to the pattern of light that produced the response. As we will see later, the responses of the so-called 'face cells' in the infero-temporal cortex suffer from the same problem of ambiguity. However, there is no need for any particular cell to signal some specific visual feature or property. We might be tempted to think that the firing of a single cell—a so-called *grandmother cell*—solves the problem of recognition of our grandmother, but remember that there is nothing 'looking at' the response of a particular single cell. The response pattern of all the cells that are activated by some particular stimulus is the signature of that particular face or any other stimulus property just as the pattern of responses of the three different types of cone receptors is the signature of the 'colour' of the light falling on that part of the retina. It is important to bear these two points in mind—the ambiguity of response of a particular single cell and relative unimportance of a cell's peak response—when considering the results of recordings from cells in other areas of the brain.

The presence of ganglion cells that have these on-centre/off-surround and off-centre/on-surround receptive field characteristics in the mammalian retina is only part of the story. Christina Enroth-Cugell and John Robson identified two different classes of ganglion cells in the cat retina: those that had sustained and approximately linear responses (such as those just described), which they termed 'X' cells, and a second class of cells that exhibited transient, non-linear responses which they referred to as 'Y' cells. The axons of these two classes of cell terminate in different layers—the parvo- and magno-cellular layers—of the LGN (lateral geniculate nucleus) (Figure 48(a)). Comparable cells in the primate visual system are referred to as 'midget' and 'parasol'. What could be the functions of these different cell types? Some have speculated that they form the basis of two separate streams that are used for processing form and motion information respectively. The small receptive field size of a typical X cell would be useful for coding detailed form whereas the transient characteristic of a typical Y cell would be useful for coding motion. This characterization of X and Y cells is almost certainly an oversimplification and provides another example of the difficulty of trying to infer function from response characteristics. All one can

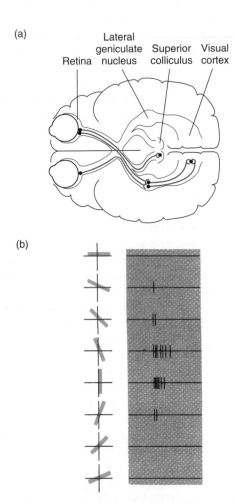

48. (a) Neural pathways from the eye to the visual cortex. (b) Hubel and Wiesel's recordings of the neural responses of 'simple' cells to bars of different orientations.

say for certain is that the X and Y ganglion cells in the cat retina, and the equivalent cells in the primate retina, act as spatio-temporal filters, with somewhat different response characteristics.

The visual cortex

At the start of the 20th century, Korbinian Brodmann showed that the outer surface of the brain, known as the cortex, is composed of many different areas including the primary visual cortex (V1). Anatomical studies have shown that the axons of LGN cells project to the different layers of the striate or primary visual cortex (Figure 48(a)). Using micro-electrodes, David Hubel and Torsten Wiesel were the first to record from individual cells in layer 4Cβ and 4A of V1 in the cat visual system, which they termed 'simple cells'. These cells were found to have receptive fields with both excitatory and inhibitory regions (like those of ganglion cells) but the simple cell receptive fields were elongated in shape rather than circular. As a consequence, the best responses of simple cells were found when the stimulus was a light bar (or line or edge) on a dark background (or vice versa) oriented at a particular angle (Figure 48(b)).

Recordings from simple cells across the surface of V1 show that the preferred orientation of simple cells changes systematically and that the cells are organized into what are referred to as *orientation columns*. Once again, some writers have wrongly assumed that the function of these cells must be as 'orientation detectors' because they respond most strongly to a preferred orientation of a line or bar, but this cannot be the case. Alan Cowey made the point that while it is true that the response of the particular simple cell is *modulated* by a change in the orientation of the line or bar (Figure 48(b)), it is also true that the response of the same cell is modulated by many other factors including the width of the bar, the length of the bar, its position, its luminance, its contrast, its wavelength, and its motion. In other words, the response of a particular simple cell is necessarily ambiguous, just like the ganglion cell responses described in this chapter. Information about orientation only exists by considering the responses of many simple cells. Once again, it is misleading to regard these cells as detectors of one particular 'feature'.

While most of the axons of X cells in the cat visual system terminate in simple cells, most of the axons of Y cells terminate in what Hubel and Wiesel referred to as 'complex cells' located in layer 4Cα in V1. The important difference between simple and complex cells is that complex cells do not have defined excitatory and inhibitory regions. In other words, a spot of light falling on different parts of a complex cell's receptive field does not produce any response. Second, complex cells typically do not respond to the presence of a stationary bar, line, or edge on the retina but instead respond only to a moving bar, line, or edge. In addition, many complex cells show directional selectivity, that is, they only respond to movement in a particular direction. Hubel and Wiesel identified a third class of V1 cell which they called 'hypercomplex' or 'end-stopped'. The best responses of hypercomplex cells differ from those of complex cells in that they only respond to a bar, line, or edge of a specific length.

The pathways of axons from V1 cells to other areas of the visual cortex can be traced using dyes that are absorbed by a cell's axon. The results reveal that there are at least two distinct neural pathways. Alan Cowey and Semir Zeki independently showed that many of the cells in the region of the primate visual cortex referred to as V4 are preferentially excited by coloured stimuli in contrast to the cells in the region referred to as V5 (or MT) that are optimally stimulated by moving stimuli. It is not surprising that cells in different areas of the visual cortex respond differently to different types of stimulation, but more recent evidence has shown that while it remains true that many of the V4 cells respond to coloured stimuli, other cells are modulated by orientation and disparity changes. Similarly, while many of the

V5/MT cells respond to moving stimuli, other cells show disparity and orientation preferences. The human brain shows a degree of functional specialization but the situation is much more complicated than the idea of separate and independent functional areas.

Two visual pathways

The discovery of separate anatomical pathways from V1 to V4 and from V1 to V5/MT has been cited as evidence of a separation into two distinct processing pathways that are referred to as the 'ventral' and 'dorsal' streams—the ventral pathway projecting downwards towards the temporal lobe and the dorsal pathway projecting upwards towards the parietal lobe (Figure 49). Leslie Ungeleider and Mort Mishkin referred to these two pathways as the 'what' and 'where' pathways on the basis of lesion experiments in monkeys. Lesions to the temporal cortex resulted in failures of object recognition whereas lesions to the parietal cortex resulted in an inability to see motion and apraxia (problems in making motor movements).

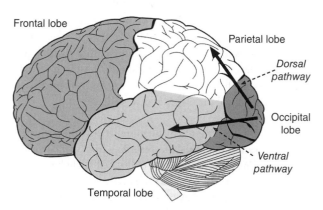

49. Ventral and dorsal pathways from V1 to the temporal lobe and parietal lobe, respectively.

More recently, David Milner and Mel Goodale have suggested that the functions of ventral and dorsal pathways are better described as the pathways for 'perception' and 'action' respectively. The existence of these two separate anatomical pathways is not in doubt but it is not clear that the functions of the two pathways are quite so distinct. Once again, it should not surprise us that different areas of the brain are involved in the processing of different types of visual information—it would be highly unlikely that the cortex is a single homogeneous structure with all areas involved in all aspects of visual processing. On the other hand, it now seems very unlikely that the processing of one particular type of information is restricted to just one specific area.

Face cells

One of the most remarkable discoveries to emerge from single cell recording comes from the work of David Perrett, Edmund Rolls, and Woody Caan who found cells in the superior temporal sulcus of the monkey brain that showed a preference for face stimuli (Figure 50(a)). When face images were presented to the monkey, some cells responded preferentially to the whole face while others showed a preference for just the eyes or just the mouths of the faces (Figure 50(b)). Moreover, a proportion of those cells showed unchanging (invariant) responses when either the orientation, colour, size, or the distance of the face from the monkey was varied. It is clear that these cells must be involved in face processing but it seems very unlikely that any single cell could uniquely signal the presence of a particular face.

Once again, it is important to distinguish between the properties of a cell that can be established by recording from that particular cell and inferring what the function of that cell might be. Identifying the properties of cells is relatively straightforward whereas determining the function of a cell is difficult if not impossible. The problem is made worse by the fact that it is impossible (in practice) to rule out the possibility that a particular

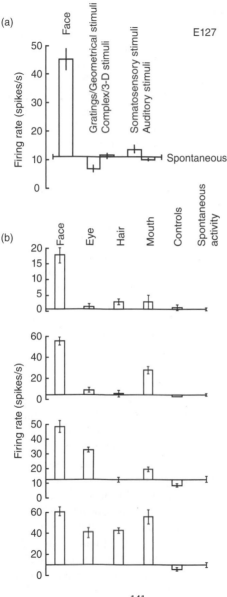

50. The neural responses to face stimuli recorded by Perrett, Rolls, and Caan in the superior temporal sulcus. (a) The firing rate was highest when faces were presented to the monkey compared to other visual stimuli. (b) *A proportion of cells only responded to complete faces (top panel) while other cells also responded to parts of the face such as the eyes, hair, or mouth (lower panels).*

141

cell might also respond to some quite different visual input without monitoring its response to an infinite number of possible stimuli. The dangers of inferring function from cell properties is further highlighted by the finding that lesions to the monkey superior temporal sulcus have little or no effect on the monkey's ability to recognize or discriminate faces. This suggests that the neural circuits involved in face identification and discrimination are not limited to a specific 'face area' in the visual cortex and it raises the more general question of whether any area of the cortex can be said to be uniquely responsible for a specific function.

The fact that these cells form part of the so-called ventral stream pathway has been used as evidence that they are part of an 'object-recognition system'. However, David Perrett has shown that some cells in this region of the superior temporal sulcus respond strongly when a monkey views a human head that rotates to face the monkey but not when the same head turns to face away from the monkey. This suggests that the role of these cells might be involved in the extraction of information about meaning (affordances) rather than recognition—a head turning towards the monkey is suggestive of a threat whereas a head turning away from the monkey is not.

Final thoughts

How should we evaluate David Marr's claim at the beginning of the chapter that we have learned 'much about the operation of the individual nerve cell, but disconcertingly little about the meaning of the circuits that they compose in the brain'? In the thirty years since he made that statement, we have certainly learned a great deal about the properties of individual neurons in the visual cortex, their interconnections, and the possible roles of different areas in the brain in different functions. VEPs (visual evoked potentials) have allowed us to monitor (non-invasively) the patterns of electrical activity created by particular visual stimuli, and the development of more powerful techniques for scanning the brain using fMRI and MEG (magneto-encephalography) have provided us with more and more precise maps of the brain regions involved in perception. Tractography, which combines fMRI techniques with sophisticated computer-based image analysis, has started to reveal the vast number of pathways (tracts) linking different areas of the brain. As a consequence, it might be thought that it is only a matter of time before we discover the 'meaning of the circuits'. However, Marr's claim was not about what might be achieved with more time or more sophisticated techniques. Rather, he was suggesting that there is a fundamental distinction between levels of explanation that cannot be easily bridged. The aims of psychological and physiological studies are different—the aim of the former is to identify whole system properties while the aim of the latter is to characterize the properties of the hardware and the mechanisms upon which our perceptual abilities are based. The results of behavioural studies may give us clues as to what to look for in the underlying neural mechanisms and the results of physiological studies may trigger interesting new thoughts about our perceptual abilities but this might not be as easy or straightforward an endeavour as some have thought.

Chapter 9
The future

What is perception?

Perception is one of the best understood topics in psychology as a result of 2,000 years of study and yet there is still no universal agreement as to how we should understand the purpose or objective of perceptual processes. Should it be to explain how we see, hear, smell, taste, and touch—our subjective experiences—or should it be to explain how sensory information guides and controls action? With respect to visual perception, it seems to me that part of the problem stems from the mistaken view that we are viewing some sort of internal picture or representation of the world and that how we behave is a consequence of 'inspecting' that internal picture. Indeed, this is how it feels. It feels as if we make our perceptual judgements on the basis of those subjective experiences, but it has to be true that the information used to make those judgements has already been extracted and, in some cases, this information has already been used to initiate the appropriate behaviour. Perhaps, one of the reasons why we have subjective experiences is that they allow us to break the normal perception–action links (that are responsible for so much of our behaviour) and to act in a different way. We might not need subjective experiences (*qualia*) in order to act in the world (as is evident from machine vision systems) but having *qualia* provides a degree of flexibility in the control of our behaviour that does not exist in the behaviour of other species.

Cognitive penetrability

There is considerable debate at present as to whether, or to what extent, our perceptual processes are *cognitively penetrable*: that is, affected by higher-level processes of attention, expectations, emotions, and knowledge. Recent evidence suggests that the so-called low-level aspects of perception are relatively unaffected by these factors but if our definition of perception involves the detection of affordances—what the world offers us—then it seems undeniable that attention, expectations, and emotions are all involved and affect our behaviour. It is also partly a matter of definition—should we see attention as a higher-level process or an intrinsic part of what it means to perceive? Indeed, is there a meaningful distinction between low-level and higher-level processes? And note that this is a question about a putative hierarchy of psychological processes, rather than about the anatomy of the underlying mechanisms. As far as 'knowledge' is concerned, it seems unlikely that our knowledge that the Moon is ~400,000 km away could have any effect on our perception of the distance to the Moon but it is undoubtedly true that our lifetime of experience (rather than knowledge) affects the way we perceive the world in a broad sense. Hopefully, some of these issues will be clarified in the future but for the present, it is important to appreciate that the different theoretical viewpoints of researchers about the nature and purpose of perception will continue to influence the sorts of experiments they carry out.

Ecological validity

One issue that will undoubtedly become more important in the future is that of ecological validity, not least because it has important consequences for the kinds of experiments we use to study perception. Simple stimuli displayed on computer screens may become part of history for several reasons. Line drawings are easy to create and manipulate, but they do not do justice to the richness of the visual information that is normally available. This brings us back to the difference between stimuli and information—manipulation of stimuli is not the same as manipulation of the relevant information. Part of the problem stems from the fact that we have adopted the strategy that has been extremely successful in the other sciences, of isolating and manipulating a single factor or variable. However, this might not be the best way of studying perception and one consequence of adopting this strategy is that we have treated the different aspects of our sensory systems as separate and independent rather than seeing them as part of a single, integrated system. When Maureen Graham and I first reported our findings on the use of motion parallax information, we entitled the paper 'Motion parallax as an *independent* cue for depth perception' (my italics). Our results revealed that motion parallax can be very effective when it is isolated from other sources of information but what we failed to appreciate was that we have evolved in a world in which there are multiple sources of information that normally function together rather than in isolation.

A related point arises from the claim that 'context affects our perceptions'—the idea that the surroundings affect the 'stimulus' we are looking at. Of course this is true, and Chapters 4 and 7 provide many examples of this happening (e.g. induced motion and other simultaneous contrast effects), but we should not assume that this is how the perceptual system parses the sensory input—into a 'stimulus' and its 'context'. The information needed to determine the lightness or colour of a surface involves making comparisons within different frames of reference. Context is not something that is 'taken into account' at a later processing stage—it is the essence of the information needed for perception, as the Gestalt psychologists proposed in the first part of the 20th century.

Comparative studies

Most of the time we suffer from a very chauvinist view of our perceptual systems—we think that what we are able to perceive represents the limits of what is available in the world. For example, it feels as if we are able to see all the shades of colour that exist in the world rather than the subset provided by our trichromatic visual systems. More importantly, we often imagine that our perceptual systems are very different from those of other species, not least because we are able to think and talk about our perceptions. However, while there are enormous differences in perceptual systems of different species, what they all share is the capacity to extract the information available in the animal's particular ecological niche that, through evolution, has been found to be important and meaningful for that particular species. It is undoubtedly true that the human perceptual system is more flexible, adaptable, and involved in a much wider variety of behaviours than the perceptual systems of other species but what we share with other species is the evolutionary legacy of exploiting the meaningful characteristics of the particular environment within the constraints of an animal's particular sensory-motor system.

Glossary

Affordances: According to Gibson, 'What the world offers us'—the 'meaning' of a pattern of sensory stimulation.

Algorithm: The procedures or rules used to transform representations.

Articulation: The degree of complexity—the number and range of different reflecting surfaces—in the surrounding lightness field.

Attuned: Gibson's idea that a perceptual system is well matched to the characteristics of the environment.

Binocular disparities: The small differences between the retinal images that are created by 3-D objects as a consequence of having two slightly different vantage points.

Biological motion: The patterns of motion of a small number of point-lights attached to the animal's limbs or joints that are created by an animal's movements.

Cognitively impenetrable: The idea that our beliefs, desires, and emotions do not affect what we perceive.

Connectionist: Neural network models of perceptual processes based on networks of units or hypothetical neurons.

Constraints: Limitations or restrictions on what is possible.

Constructivist: Perceptual theory that involves the need to construct or reconstruct our perceptions from limited sensory information.

Demand characteristics: Koffka's idea that the value of a thing can be directly perceived.

Deuteranopia: Absence of the medium wavelength cones.

Differential perspective: The differences in the perspective projections to the two eyes as a result of having two spatially separated vantage points.

Direct perception: Gibson's idea that there is sufficient information in the sensory input that can be 'picked up' without the need for elaboration or embellishment.

Distributed or ensemble coding: The idea that the coding of a particular sensory characteristic, e.g. orientation of a line, is signalled by the distribution of activity over a number of neurons rather than present in the activity of a single neuron.

Equivalent configurations: The many different real-world scenes that can create the same retinal image.

Explicit: Marr's idea that although a particular visual feature such as an edge is present in an image, there needs to be a mechanism to extract that feature and make it explicit.

Exterospecific information: Information about characteristics of the environment.

Grandmother cell: The idea that there could be a particular cell in the visual cortex that responded to a particular visual input such as one's grandmother.

Indirect theories: Theories claiming that perception involves higher-level processes of enrichment or embellishment that add 'meaning' to the sensory input.

Induced motion: The impression of motion in a stationary object as a result of motion in the surrounding region.

Information: Gibson's use of the term information refers to the 'specification of the environment'.

Invariants: The things that do not change—e.g. the size of an object changes with its distance from the observer but the relative sizes of two objects stay the same.

Inverse optics: The problem of how we can determine which particular 3-D world scene produced a given 2-D retinal image.

Inverse square law: The law describing how binocular disparities decrease with the square of the distance from the observer.

Lambertian: An ideal, diffusely reflecting surface.

Lateral inhibition: The activity of a particular cell is affected by the activity of neighbouring cells. First observed in the horseshoe crab Limulus.

Lightness: Perceived reflectance—white, black, or a shade of grey.

Lightness records: The spatial patterns of relative reflectances under long, medium, and short wavelength light.

Local sign: Each receptor in the retina is assumed to have a unique local sign specifying the visual direction of light falling on that receptor with respect to the eye.

Metamerism: Perceptually indistinguishable mixtures of stimuli, e.g. in colour vision where different combinations of wavelengths are seen as the same.

Micropsia: The appearance of objects as being smaller than they actually are.

Motion parallax: The relative motion in the optic array or retinal image created by points or surfaces located at different distances during observer or object movement.

Motion perspective: The gradients of relative motion in the optic array or retinal image created by the 3-D surfaces during observer or object movement.

Optic array: A description of how light is structured at a particular vantage point.

Optic flow: The changing pattern of light at a particular vantage point, or on the retina, as a result of observer or object motion.

Orientation columns: Systematically organized columns of neurons that respond to lines (or edges) of particular orientations.

Perceptions: For Helmholtz, perceptions are thought to be a consequence of 'higher-level' processes that give sensations their meaning.

Perceptual information: Gibson's use of the term perceptual information refers to the 'specification of the environment'.

Perceptual system: Gibson's idea that sensory and motor systems are not distinct but rather part of an overall perceptual system.

Prior: The a priori probability of the particular state that is an essential part of Bayesian inference.

Propriospecific: Information about positions and movements of the observer.

Protanopia: Absence of the long wavelength cones.

Qualia: Our subjective, conscious experiences, e.g. our experience of the colour red.

Receptive field: The area of the retina where visual stimulation can cause a change in the response of a particular neuron.

Representation: According to Marr, a formal system for making *explicit* certain entities or types of information.

Retinex: Land's model of colour perception based on the comparison of three lightness records.

Sensations: The outputs of low-level sensory mechanisms.

Sequence models: Models of motion perception that involve detecting the sequential activity in spatially separated receptors.

Smart perceptual mechanisms: Runeson's idea of a mechanism that can directly signal some perceptual characteristic of the world without the need for calculations or computations.

Species-specific: For Gibson, perceptual information—the specification of the environment—is different for different species.

Spectral sensitivity function: The function describing the sensitivity of a particular receptor to different wavelengths of light.

Stimulus: The energy impinging on a sensory receptor.

Temporal correlation: The correlation between events happening at different points in time as in the detection of motion using spatially separated receptors.

Tritanopia: Absence of the short wavelength cones.

Vantage point: A particular viewing position.

Vertical disparity: The difference in the vertical positions of a point projected on the retinas of the two eyes.

Visual cliff: The apparatus used in Gibson and Walk's experiment in which there was a sudden, visually specified drop from an upper platform to a lower surface.

Visual direction: The direction of an object with respect to the eye.

Whole-system: The properties of the complete perceptual system that may be revealed using behavioural or psychophysical techniques.

Further reading

Chapter 1: What is perception?

R. L. Gregory (1998). *Eye and Brain* (5th edition). Oxford University Press.

H. von Helmholtz (1910). *Physiological Optics*. Dover.

Chapter 2: Perceptual theories—direct, indirect, and computational

I. Rock (1983). *The Logic of Perception* (1983). MIT Press.

J. J. Gibson (1979). *The Ecological Approach to Visual Perception*. Houghton Mifflin.

D. Marr (1982). *Vision*. Freeman.

S. Ullman (1980). 'Against direct perception'. *Behavioural and Brain Sciences*, 3: 373–415.

Chapter 3: Lightness and colour

A. Gilchrist (2006). *Seeing Black and White*. Oxford University Press.

B. A. Wandell (1995). *Foundations of Vision*. Sinauer Associates.

E. H. Land (1977). 'The retinex theory of color vision'. *Scientific American*, 237: 108–28.

Chapter 4: Motion perception

G. Mather (2009). *Foundations of Perception* (2nd edition). Psychology Press.

V. Bruce, P. R. Green, and M. A. Georgeson (2003). *Visual Perception: Physiology, Psychology and Ecology* (4th edition). Psychology Press.

Chapter 5: Perception of a 3-D world

I. P. Howard and B. J. Rogers (1995). *Binocular Vision and Stereopsis*. Oxford University Press.

G. Mather (2009). *Foundations of Perception* (2nd edition). Psychology Press.

D. C. Knill and W. Richards (1996). *Perception as Bayesian Inference*. Cambridge University Press.

Chapter 6: Perception and action

J. J. Gibson (1979). *The Ecological Approach to Visual Perception*. Houghton Mifflin.

V. Bruce, P. R. Green, and M. A. Georgeson (2003). *Visual Perception: Physiology, Psychology and Ecology* (4th edition). Psychology Press.

M. F. Land and B. W Tatler (2009). *Looking and Acting*. Oxford University Press.

Chapter 7: Delusions about illusions

R. L. Gregory (2009). *Seeing through Illusions*. Oxford University Press.

B. J. Rogers (2017). 'Where have all the illusions gone', in A. G. Shapiro and D. Todorovic (eds), *The Oxford Compendium of Visual Illusions*. Oxford University Press.

B. Gillam (1998). 'Illusions at century's end', in J. Hochberg (ed.), *Perception and Cognition at Century's End*. Academic Press.

Chapter 8: The physiology and anatomy of the visual system

D. H. Hubel (2005). *Eye, Brain, and Vision* (2nd edition). Scientific American Library.

A. D. Milner and M. A. Goodale (2006). *The Visual Brain in Action* (2nd edition). Oxford University Press.

M. R. Bennett and P. M. S. Hacker (2003). *Philosophical Foundations of Neuroscience*. Blackwell Publishing.

Chapter 9: The future

T. J. Lombardo (1987). *The Reciprocity of Perceiver and Environment*. Lawrence Erlbaum Associates.

J. J. Koenderink (2014). 'The All Seeing Eye?'. *Perception*, 43: 1–6.

Index